A History of Belize

Nation in the making

Published by Cubola Productions
35 Elizabeth Street
Benque Viejo del Carmen
Belize, C.A.

Design by A to Z Graphic Studio
Illustrations by Rachael Heusner

Edited by Robert Leslie

We are grateful to the Education Development Centre, Ministry of Education for their helpful comments to the manuscript, to Yasser Musa for his contribution to the Cultural Freedom section and to Geraldine Holland, Leonardo Manzanero, Carmita Ruiz, David Ruiz and Vivianni Teul for the development of students' activities.

Photographs by: Mina Bárcenas, Belize National Archives, Cubola Archives, Government Information Service, Mexican Embassy, Ygnacio Rivero and the University College of Belize.

First revised edition, July 1995
14th revised edition, June 2013

Printed and bound in Mexico

ISBN 976-8142-09-X

A History of Belize

Nation in the making

Part One
Colonialism in Belize

FROM THE 15TH CENTURY onwards, nations in Europe began to conquer and settle the Americas as part of a world-wide **process** in which they also controlled Africa, Asia and Oceania. This system of taking control of foreign land is called **colonialism**. At this time European societies were developing and expanding very fast.

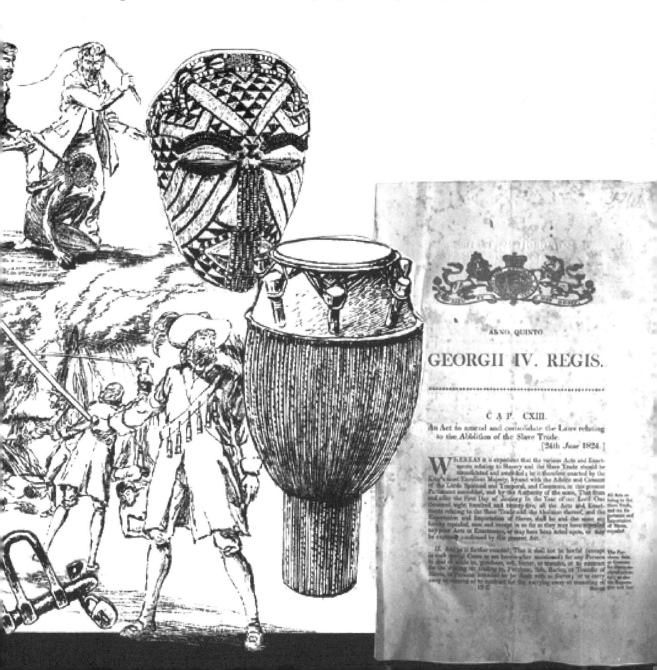

Explorations were launched in search of more wealth and **resources**. Europeans took control of the land and riches, and forced the indigenous people to work for them. In the Americas millions of the original population died from wars and disease. Later, European settlers and people from Africa and Asia were brought to work for the colonizers.

The colonization of Belize by the British was part of this world-wide process. In addition to its indigenous inhabitants, Belizeans are now a mixture of people from many parts of the world: from Europe, Africa, and Asia as well as the Americas.

In Part One we will study the growth of European colonization and its impact on the Caribbean and Belize. We will also look at the slave trade and the system of slavery. But first, we will find out who the original people of Belize were before the Europeans came.

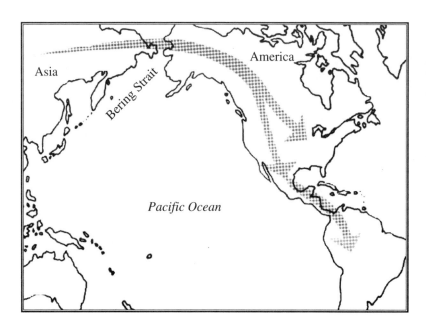

The first Americans came from Asia across the Bering Strait.

Chapter 1:
The First People of the Americas

When the Europeans came to the Americas in the 15th century, there were about thirty million people living in this **hemisphere**. These people were of very different **cultures** and lived in varied and separate societies. Some societies were as complex as the Aztecs, whose large cities were supported by innovative agricultural methods; or the magnificent mountain cities of the Incas, who practiced terrace cultivation.

The first inhabitants of the Americas appeared about 50,000 years ago. At that time the Bering Strait between Asia and North America was not covered by water. Scientists believe that over a period of several thousand years people from Asia travelled east over this passage. In their search for food, they probably followed herds of animals to what is now the Americas. These newcomers were the **ancestors** of the **indigenous** people of the Americas. Their **descendants** slowly travelled south, making homes all over the continent. After thousands of years they adapted to their different **environments**, learned new skills, created new traditions and developed diverse cultures. By the time the Europeans came, various peoples occupied different areas of the Americas – for example, the Iroquois in the northeast, the Navahos in the southwest and the Cherokees in the southeast of what is now the United States of America.

American-Indian girl.

Who were the ancestors of the indigenous people of the Americas. Who are their descendants?

Indigenous people in Brazil were very skilled with bows and arrows.

7

We know these people had many skills which they used to survive and communicate. They knew how to use fire and they made tools out of bone, wood and stone. They were good hunters and made clothing from the skins of animals.

Farming and Settling

Some of the early settlers in the Caribbean and Central America were the Arawaks and Caribs. They were skilled hunters and fishermen who caught birds, fish, turtles and other animals.

The Arawaks were also farmers. Like other groups in the Americas, they learned how to farm about 9,000 years ago. It was an important development when they learned not only the different uses of wild seeds, fruits, and roots, but also how to **cultivate** them. Some of the crops grown by the early peoples of the Caribbean were yam, cassava, maize, tobacco and cotton.

As these people became better farmers, they began to settle down and live in one place instead of travelling to find food. Now they had more time to develop new skills such as weaving and pottery making.

In what is today Central America and Mexico, the Maya developed complex civilizations. This took place thousands of years before the Europeans came and called this continent a "new world".

Pottery from
North America.

Peruvian
textile.

The Maya

The Maya lived in the area that is now southern Mexico, Guatemala, northern Honduras, El Salvador, and Belize. The peak of the Maya civilization was between 250 A.D. and 900 A.D. But it took thousands of years to develop.

The Maya grew corn, beans, squash, cocoa and chile peppers. They learned to make clay pots, hardened by fire, that were both useful and beautiful. They cultivated cotton and learned to dye and weave cloth in bright patterns. They constructed buildings and created sculptures from stone. They made jewelry and ornaments from jade, and traded gold, silver, copper and bronze with other peoples.

The earliest known settled community in the Maya world is Cuello in the Orange Walk District. Cuello existed as long ago as 2,000 B.C. The Maya of Cuello were great pottery makers and farmers.

Eventually many communities in the Maya world grew and became more complex. Great cities flourished. The Maya built grand temples, palaces and public buildings, plazas and ball courts, and created sculptures that showed the lives of their gods and heroes. Many people came to these cities to trade and worship. This period of development between 250 A.D. to 1,000 A.D. became known as the Classic Period of the Maya. Among the communities that became powerful civic centres at this time in Belize were Altun Ha, Lubaantun, El Pilar, Xunantunich and Caracol.

Maya vessel.

Pre-columbian figure of a young girl.

The Maya ceremonial centre of Cahal Pech.

9

Religion, mathematics and astronomy played an important role in the culture of the Maya. All these were closely connected. The priests were also astronomers and very active in public affairs. Many of their most important buildings were devoted to these activities. With these combined skills, the Maya were able to make calendars that were far more complicated than those we have today, and just as accurate.

The Maya had a system of writing. They recorded important events on big slabs of stone called stela. These writings are still visible 2,000 years later and are helping us to discover more about their culture. Writing was also set down in books made from bark. Very few of these pages have survived to this day. Most of the books were burned when the colonizers arrived because the symbols and their meanings seemed evil to the Spanish priests.

There is still much we do not know about Maya society, but every year **archaeologists** make new discoveries among the ruins of the ancient cities. We do know that each city was largely independent but often they would go to war to expand their control and influence to other cities. Maya society was divided into strictly ranked groups. Each group had its own rights and duties. At the top were the supreme rulers who inherited their position. The merchants were also important to Maya society. They traded by sea and by land. They traded salt, cotton, cocoa, fish, honey, feathers, shells and precious stones. Cocoa beans were used as money. Belize was an important trading centre for the entire Maya area. Some major trading centres were Moho Caye, Santa Rita, Ambergris Caye and Wild Cane Caye.

The majority of the Maya were farmers. They lived in simple thatched houses surrounded by forest gardens. They ate tortillas, beans, tomatoes, peppers and other vegetables. The rich had a more elaborate diet of turkey, fish and game meat, and a chocolate drink made of cocoa and chile. Most Maya wore simple cotton clothes and occasionally sandals. The rulers and merchants wore jewelry and feathered headbands.

Maya stela.

🖋 *Look at the drawing on page 10. Write a short description of what you observe.*

🖋🖋 *Bring photographs or make drawings depicting ancient Maya culture.*

🖋🖋 *Find out the differences in the social structure of Maya society. Make a diagram showing the hierarchy.*

Young Maya girls from southern Belize.

All civilizations have periods of growth and decline. By the middle of the 10th century, Maya society began to decline rapidly. Although the causes are not certain, archaeologists believe this may have happened because the land was no longer able to produce enough food for the people. Changes in climate, wars and scarcity of products to trade may have further contributed to weaken Maya society. As temples and public buildings were abandoned they began to decay. Many people moved to other areas. The population became smaller. Yet there were still many Maya in Belize by the 16th and 17th centuries. They had been there since ancient times, and survived the decline of their great civilization. But when the Europeans arrived and began to colonize the land, Maya civilization was dealt yet another blow.

Today the indigenous Maya live in areas of Guatemala, Mexico and Belize. They speak twenty-four Maya languages that evolved from the Classic times.

Let us now look at how the Europeans came and colonized the Americas.

Research on theories apart from those mentioned in the text, on the cause of decline of the Maya society. make drawings to illustrate these.

Where in Belize can you find Maya communities today? Find out which Maya languages are spoken. Find out a few words and their meanings.

Chapter 2:
European Rivalries in the Caribbean

From the 15th century onwards, European countries like Portugal, Spain, the Netherlands, France and Britain began to build **empires** around the world. These nations expanded their political control, their economic systems and their cultural influence in Africa, Asia, Oceania and the Americas.

The port of Sevilla in Spain. Many expeditions to the "new world" set off from this port.

Portuguese sailors and navigators were among the first to set out on remarkable voyages of exploration. In 1415, the Portuguese captured the city of Cueta in North Africa. They then went on to conquer the West African coast that was rich in gold, ivory and silver. In 1498, an explorer named Vasco da Gama sailed around the Cape of Good Hope, going around the continent of Africa for the first time in history. This opened up a sea route to India for Europe.

While the Portuguese explored the east, the Spanish set out to explore the oceans to the west. Encouraged by an Arabian idea that the world was round, Christopher Columbus sailed from Spain in 1492, hoping to reach China and India. After a hazardous ten-week voyage, he sighted the Bahamas on October 12, l492. To the Europeans this was a new world. But Columbus at first thought he had reached India. It is because of this mistake that we still call the people who first lived in the Americas "Indians" and the islands in the Caribbean the "West Indies". The Continent itself was later named America after another explorer, Amerigo Vespucci, who reached this "new world" in 1499.

Christopher Columbus.

British Supremacy in the Caribbean

It was the Spanish ships the "Pinta", the "Niña" and the "Santa Maria" that first landed in the Caribbean. Spain wanted absolute control over the "New World". They wanted only Spanish people, Spanish trade, Spanish religion and Spanish government to control the lands and bring riches of gold home. Spain defended its **monopoly** by destroying the island peoples such as the Arawaks and the Caribs. They also conquered the great Aztec and Inca civilizations on the mainland.

 Draw a map showing Christopher Columbus' route to the "new world".

 Read the chapter and make a list of some important events that took place in the 15th century.

 Locate on a world map the countries that began to build empires in the 15th century. How did these countries build their empires?

The Spanish treated the Amerindians cruelly.

The riches of this new world, however, attracted other European powers. The British, Dutch and French challenged Spain's monopoly in the 17th century. They used piracy, smuggling, and outright war to take over lands and set up their own colonies.

The Dutch, for example, took Guiana, and the British captured St. Kitts, Barbados and Jamaica from Spain. In the middle of the 17th century, some British pirates settled among logwood forests on the coast of the Bay of Honduras – what would later be called the Settlement of Belize. The French were also settling in North America and the Caribbean.

Naval battle.

In the 18th century, the British and French fought for supremacy over the "New World". The British took control of more and more territories in the Caribbean. By the 19th century the British were the major power in the Caribbean. The British empire extended to all parts of the world, including the Americas, Africa, India, Asia and Oceania.

In the centuries that followed the great powers of Europe struggled with each other in heated and often violent rivalry to build their huge world empires.

Describe the naval battle in the picture. What do you think they were fighting for? Notice that the ships had only sails, sometimes the weather was bad. Write a story about how you would had felt if you had been there.

A British pirate.

15

Chapter 3:
The Spanish and British in Belize

In 1519-20, Hernan Cortes conquered the Aztec empire in Mexico. His lieutenant, Pedro de Alvarado, defeated the Maya in Yucatan. Expeditions were sent to conquer what is now Guatemala and Honduras. Cortes himself passed through the south-west corner of the Toledo District in 1525. Scattered settlements of Mopan and Chol Maya in that area were also devastated by Spanish **incursions** in the 17th century.

The Spaniards tried to control the Maya of Chetumal. Chetumal was then the capital of a large Maya area, and was located just west of present-day Corozal Town, possibly at Santa Rita. In answer to a demand to submit to Spain, Chetumal's chief, Nachankan, replied that his only **tribute** would be "turkeys in the shape of spears and corn in the shape of arrows". The Maya defeated the Spanish and old Chetumal in Belize became a place of refuge for Maya fleeing the Spanish rule.

The Spanish invaders moved farther south, but all attempts to control other Maya villages, like Lamanai in New River Lagoon, and Tipu, a Maya village of about 500 inhabitants near Negroman in the Cayo District, eventually failed. The Maya fought back. They burnt the churches the Spanish missionaries had built and returned to their old beliefs. In southern Belize, the Chol Maya opposed the Spanish in the same manner.

The Spanish never had lasting control over the Maya in Belize. They never settled in the area but they did cause social disruption. During the Classic Period of the Maya, the population of what is now Belize was at least 400,000. After the decline, the population was greatly reduced. Of those who remained, as much as 86 per cent died after coming into contact with the Spanish. Some were killed in war, but most of them died from new European diseases brought by the conquerors.

Observe the drawing on page 16. How would you describe Spanish dominance over the Maya?

What were some of the major causes that reduced the Maya population in Belize?

Look at the population map in the Atlas of Belize. Trace a map and the route that the Spanish missionaries would follow from Bacalar, in Mexico, to Tipu following the course of several rivers.

At first, the buccaneers were hunters. Pressured by Spanish aggressions, they turned to piracy.

By the time the British came to Belize the Maya were no longer living near the coast. When the British arrived in the 17th century they did not mention any contact with the Maya. It was only late in the 18th century that their records show contact with the Maya inland.

British Settlers

The first British who arrived on the coast of Belize left few records. They were pirates, buccaneers and adventurers, and lived in rough camps which they used as bases to raid Spanish ships. By the middle of the 17th century these pirates began to cut the logwood they found in the area. In 1670 the Treaty of Madrid put an end to the piracy and encouraged these settlers to cut logwood. These settlers were called Baymen.

Logwood is a tree from which a valuable dye used to colour woolen cloth was made. It was the economic basis for the British settlement in Belize for over 100 years.

Spain versus Britain

There was frequent conflict between the British and the Spanish over the right of the British to settle in Belize and cut logwood. During the 18th century the Spanish attacked the settlement many times, and in 1717, 1730, 1754 and 1779 forced the settlers to leave. However, the Spanish never settled in Belize, and the British returned and expanded their settlements and trade.

In 1763, the Treaty of Paris gave the British rights to cut and export logwood. But Spain still claimed **sovereignty** over the land. By this time the logwood trade declined, but the mahogany trade started to grow, and the Baymen continued to log the area.

On September 15, 1779 the Spanish captured St. George's Caye, where most of the settlers lived. One hundred and forty prisoners and 250 slaves were captured and shipped to Havana. The settlement was deserted until a new peace was declared in 1783. By that time, mahogany had become the major export.

✎ Find out the meaning of "buccaneer".

✎✎ Make a time line to show the Treaties between Spain and Great Britain, and Spanish attacks to the Settlement from 1670 until the Battle of St. George's Caye. What can you learn from this time line?

✎✎ Find out where in Belize is logwood still found.

New agreements continued to be made between the Spanish and British about the rights of the Baymen. The Treaty of Versailles, in 1783, gave the British rights to cut only logwood. It allowed them to cut trees between the Hondo and Belize rivers, with the New River as the western boundary. The settlers **petitioned** the British government, and a new agreement was signed in 1786.

This Convention permitted the Baymen to cut both logwood and mahogany as far as the Sibun River. But they were not allowed to build forts, to govern themselves, engage in agriculture, or do any work other than woodcutting. In addition, this Convention gave the Spanish the right to **inspect** the settlement.

Grave of Thomas Pott, a renowned settler of the Bay of Honduras, at St. George's Caye.

The British continued to have only limited rights over the area. Then on September 10, 1798 there was another Spanish attack on the Settlement of Belize. The Spanish forces were strong, but the Baymen were more familiar with the coastal waters. This time, with the help of their African slaves, an armed **sloop**, and three companies of a West Indian Regiment, the British side won what became known as the Battle of St. George's Caye. The Spanish retreated and never again tried to control Belize.

The British versus the Maya

In the past, some historians claimed that when the British settlers came in the 17th century, Belize was **uninhabited**. But we have seen that the Maya still lived in the area. As the British moved deeper into the interior they came into contact with them.

Divide into two groups: one group is to represent the Maya's perspective; the other, the British settlers' perspective. Discuss the issue of Maya resistance.

The Maya strongly resisted British attempts to take over their territory. In 1788, the British reported a Maya attack on woodcutters at New River. In 1802 some troops were ordered to "be sent up river to punish the Indians who are committing depredations upon the mahogany works". There were many such conflicts throughout the 19th century.

Despite their strong resistance, the Maya were forced back by the British. By 1839, they had retreated into the forests around San Ignacio. But they did not stop fighting. The Maya continued to attack mahogany camps and to control inland areas of Belize.

The Maya of Yucatan fought Spanish colonization well into the 20th century.

Remains of Corozal Fort.

Many Mestizo families came to Belize as refugees from the Caste Wars.

In 1866, the Maya leader Marcos Canul led a raid on a mahogany camp at Qualm Hill on the Rio Bravo in what is today the Orange Walk District. Two men died and a ransom was demanded for the captured prisoners. The Maya also demanded rent to be paid for the use of the land the British occupied. Later that year Canul's army defeated a detachment of British troops. Five British soldiers were killed and 16 wounded.

The settlers were very scared. The British sent more troops and weapons, went into Maya villages and burnt their houses and fields. Their intention was to drive the Maya out by destroying their food supplies. Over the next five years the Maya rebuilt their villages and replanted their fields. Canul and his men continued to fight. In 1870 they took over Corozal Town. In 1872 they attacked the British barracks at Orange Walk, New River but they could not capture it. Canul was mortally wounded, and they retreated. This was the last major Maya attack on the British.

The British had been determined to get the Maya from their lands so they could cut mahogany in the areas surrounding the colony. They saw them as an obstacle to their mahogany business. They felt the Maya could provide them with cheap labour, and tried to prevent them from owing land. In 1867, Governor Austin ruled that "No Indians will be at liberty to reside upon or occupy or cultivate any land without previous payment or engagement to pay rent whether to the Crown or the owner of the land".

Write a short paragraph to describe the personality of Maya leader Marcos Canul.

Discuss Governor Austin's rule.

Make a drawing of the Battle of Orange Walk. Before you start, find out about the landscape features of the area.

21

Chapter 4:
Slavery and the Slave Trade

The British woodcutters who settled Belize in the 18th century soon looked for people who could work for them. They could not find enough labourers locally, and so they began to use the same source of labour used in the sugar plantations of the Caribbean – slaves from Africa.

Slavery is a system in which human beings are owned and forced to work by their master. Slaves can be bought and sold, and are denied all rights, even to have a say about what happens to their children.

Slavery has existed throughout history, in societies as varied as those of Rome, China and Africa. Many kinds of people in history have been, at some time or another, both slaves and slave owners. But in the Americas there developed a system of slavery that was closely associated with race – almost always, the masters were white and the slaves black. The child of a slave mother was born into slavery, and generally a black person was assumed to be a slave until he or she could prove otherwise. Slavery was built upon the unjustifiable theory that black people were inferior to white people. Because of this, several generations remained in bondage. Racism was used even after slavery to continue the abuse and **discrimination** of people, simply because of the colour of their skin.

Branding irons, manacles, and fetters were used to transport and punish slaves.

A Labour Force for the Americas

The Europeans severely reduced the population of the Caribbean through war and disease. When they began to use the lands to grow sugar and tobacco and other crops, they needed workers. They took the lands of the indigenous people and forced them to do the work. As the plantations grew larger and larger, more people were needed.

They then looked for white labour. Convicts from Europe were sent to the Caribbean and forced to work. Poor white people came from Europe as **"indentured servants"**. However, there were not enough Europeans who were willing to come to the Americas under these conditions.

In the 15th century the Portuguese began slave trading with Africa. Europeans in the Americas now became involved in this trade to satisfy their need for workers.

The African Slave Trade

Slavery existed in Africa long before the Portuguese arrived. Captured prisoners from wars between the tribes in Africa were often kept as slaves. A slave trade existed within Africa and with East India as early as the 12th century.

The trade in Africans across the Atlantic Ocean began in the early 16th century and continued for almost 350 years. The Europeans made huge profits from this trade. It helped to expand and enrich their economies.

In 1518, the first African slaves arrived in the Americas. They came to Hispaniola from Guinea in West Africa. What began as simply trade in gold, ivory, pepper, and only a few human beings, became a huge trade in human **cargo** in the 17th, 18th and 19th centuries. The slave trade was part of a triangular trade route. Manufactured goods were taken from Europe to Africa. The goods were exchanged for slaves who were then taken to the Americas. There the slaves were exchanged for sugar and other colonial products which were shipped back to Europe. Many people were involved in this profitable trade, from European and Arabian merchants to African kings.

TO BE SOLD on board the Ship Bance-Island, on tuesday the 6th of May next, at Ashley-Ferry; a choice cargo of about 250 fine healthy NEGROES, just arrived from the Windward & Rice Coast. —The utmost care has already been taken, and shall be continued, to keep them free from the least danger of being infected with the SMALL-POX, no boat having been on board, and all other communication with people from Charles-Town prevented.

Austin, Laurens, & Appleby.

N. B. Full one Half of the above Negroes have had the SMALL-POX in their own Country.

Posters were printed to announce the sale of slaves on arrival.

In your opinion, what is discrimination? Do you think it still exists today? Discuss it with your class.

Locate on a map the areas of the world that were involved in the triangular trade. Draw a diagram showing the route.

The trade in Africans across the Atlantic was the largest and most terrible experience of forced human **migration** the world has ever known. During the 300-year period of slavery, between 15 and 20 million Africans were transported. Millions of Africans were forced to suffer the nightmarish trip into slavery across the Atlantic. This voyage across the Atlantic, the middle stage in the trading triangle, was called the Middle Passage.

People were captured and traded in Africa, then crowded into pens, called baracoons, like cattle. Many died before they even boarded the ships. Once on board, the slaves were so crowded and provided with so little food and water that they often became sick and died. It was common for about a third of the number on a ship to die before they reached the Americas. One ship, the "Hannibal", lost 320 of its 700 slaves. The captain complained about his own "misery", "pain", and "ruin", because he lost so much of his cargo.

While millions of Africans were being enslaved in the Americas, the proud and ancient peoples of Africa were also being conquered and colonized and their cultures destroyed.

The drawing tells us the story of a young man captured in Africa by the slave traders. Write the story giving the characters African names.

An African's View of Slavery

from the autobiography of the ex-slave Equiano:

Forced on Board: *When I looked round the ship too and saw ... a multitude of black people of every description chained together, everyone of their countenances expressing dejection and sorrow, I no longer doubted my fate.*

The Middle Passage: *The stench of the hold while we were on the coast was so intolerably loathsome that it was dangerous to remain there for any length of time, and some of us had been permitted to stay on the deck for fresh air; but now that the whole ship's cargo were confined together it became absolutely pestilential. The closeness of the place and the heat of the climate, added to the number in the ship, which was so crowded that each had scarcely room to turn himself, almost suffocated us.*

Sold in the Americas: *On a signal given (at the beat of a drum) the buyers rush at once into the yard where the slaves are confined, and make choices of that parcel they like best. The noise and the clamour with which this is attested and the eagerness visible in the countenances of the buyers serve not a little to increase the apprehensions of the terrified Africans ... In this manner without scruple, are relations and friends separated, most of them never to see each other again. In such a state, of mixed fear and grief, ill-health and terror, the Africans are taken away by their masters, strangers in a strange land.*

Drawing of the hull of a ship used to carry slaves. Slaves were crammed together with scarcely any room to turn.

The Africans

The earliest human beings appeared in Asia and Africa. Discoveries in eastern and southern Africa show that tool-making peoples lived there more than 500,000 years ago. Like every early civilization around the world they discovered fire, learned to hunt, and cultivated crops.

African hunter-gatherers later became farmers and cattlemen. Around 500 B.C., stone tools and weapons were gradually replaced by iron. This improved their ways of working and fighting so quickly that in a few hundred years different African peoples developed advanced civilizations. Some cultures became skilled metalworkers in gold, copper, tin and bronze. In time, powerful kingdoms and empires were formed. All these developments took place almost 2,000 years before the European slave trade.

African Life

Ancestors played an important part in the lives of African people. They felt that their ancestors could still influence their lives for good or bad. Elders and priests reminded the people of their ancient customs and traditions and they were advisors to the kings. They were also the judges, the medicine men, and the religious leaders.

Although African religions are very different from one another, they are similar in many ways. African religions, like many others, believed in many gods. Each god had special powers, or watched over a special activity. Each craft and trade had its own god. There were also the gods of the earth, sky, and the sun.

Music was closely connected with the religious traditions. Two important features of African music were intricate rhythms and call and response compositions, where the leader sings, then the chorus sings back.

Music festivals were used to celebrate important social and religious events. Drums were used to communicate from one village to the next. These were called "talking drums". Even today Africans have many different kinds of drums. A wide variety of instruments were used in addition to drums, such as banjos, castanets, clarinets, trumpets, fiddles, fifes, flutes, rattles, tambourines and triangles.

The slave trade destroyed the wealth and property in African societies, but most Africans kept their cultural heritage. Those who came to the Americas brought their culture with them.

**African woman
from Nigeria**

In which parts of Belize is African culture alive? Name some of the African influences in our culture.

Compose a song with a call and response pattern. Use percussion, rattles and voice. Make simple instruments using recycled materials like cans and natural materials such as gourds or bambu filled with pebbles. Study the illustration for more ideas.

Folk shawm *Friction instrument* *Xylophone* *Sistrum* *Rattle* *Footed drum* *Simple zither* *Goblet drum* *Clapper bells* *Folk lute* *Slit drum* *Barrel drum*

Chapter 5:
Slavery in Belize

Logging in the forests of Belize.

Throughout the Caribbean, slavery was associated with sugar plantations. Sugar production made each island a single-crop economy, entirely dependent upon colonial trade. Large numbers of slaves worked on huge plantations and slave communities developed. As the slave population increased, large black majorities developed who were ruled by white minorities. This became the typical Caribbean society, divided by race, culture, and class.

In Belize, slaves were used for logging. Therefore, slavery and Belizean society developed differently from other parts of the Caribbean where slaves and their families worked and lived in plantations. Slaves in Belize worked in scattered gangs in the forests, separated from their families in Belize City.

But there were similarities. Belizean masters had control over the lives of their slaves, and treated them like mere property. But because of the kind of work they did slaves were able to maintain some control over their lives.

Slaves were auctioned on arrival, and families were often separated.

Origins

The earliest historical record of black slaves is from a Spanish missionary in 1724. He reported that they had been "introduced but a short time before from Jamaica and Bermuda".

Most of the slaves were brought to Belize in the late 18th century from the West Indies. Often they came through markets in Jamaica but some were brought directly from Africa, or from the United States. At that time most of the slaves bought by the British were taken from the Niger and Cross Delta regions in the Bight of Benin (present-day Nigeria) in West Africa, and from further south in the Congo and Angola.

In 1850, African slaves in Belize still identified themselves according to the tribes they came from in Africa. It was stated that there were in Belize "Congoes, Nangoes, Mongolas, Ashantees, Eboes, and other African tribes". One section of Belize Town was known throughout the first half of the 19th century as Eboe Town. In 1850 it was said to consist of "numerous yards, flanked with long rows of what are called negro houses, being simply separate rooms under one roof, which used to be appropriated to slaves, and now accommodate the poorer labourers".

Observe the illustration in page 28. Write a play about a slave auction and dramatize it.

Find out words of African languages that have survived in the Creole language.

St. John's Cathedral, was built by slaves in 1812.

A 1912 view of Belize City with wooden bridge across the Haulover Creek.

Population

African slaves were the majority of the population before the middle of the 18th century. An early **census** in 1790 showed that three quarters of the population were slaves, a tenth white, and the rest were free blacks and people of mixed races. Hundreds more slaves were brought to Belize before the slave trade was ended in 1807. But in the next 25 years the number of slaves declined from about 3,000 to 2,000, or from about three quarters to less than half of the population. This was because the free black and coloured population increased to almost half. The white population stayed at about one tenth of the total.

As long as slaves were imported into Belize their number increased. But after the **abolition** of the slave trade the numbers declined, in part because of the high death rates and low birth rates. The slaves died from disease, **malnutrition**, ill-treatment, over-work and accidents; sometimes they killed themselves. The birth rates were low because there were generally two or three men to every woman. Abortion was probably common because slave women did not wish to have their children born slaves. In addition, there were large numbers of slaves who escaped from the settlement. Between 1807 and 1834 approximately 200 slaves escaped. About 600 slaves gained their freedom in that period.

But, as in other parts of the Caribbean, slaves died mainly because of the horrible living conditions under slavery. Their populations were maintained only by the slave trade.

Make two pie charts. One showing the composition of Belize's population in 1790 and the other to show the composition twenty-five years later.

Name two circumstances that can cause a person to be malnourished.

A thread-wheel in Jamaica used for the punishment of slaves.

Belize River. The logs were trimmed and floated downstream to Belize Town.

Woodcutting

Slaves in Belize were initially used to cut logwood. Because of the way logwood was cut, a large number of small timber works developed along rivers, creeks, and lagoons in unsettled areas. The white settlers, with only one or two slaves, cut the logwood themselves.

When the settlers began to cut mahogany instead of logwood they needed more money, land, and workers. Mahogany trees were larger and grew farther inland and farther from each other than logwood. After 1770, 80 per cent of all male slaves aged ten years or older logged mahogany.

Woodcutting was seasonal and required the workers to spend long periods of time isolated in camps, away from their families. The mahogany trees had to be found, cut, and trimmed. Then logs were taken through temporary paths to the nearest riverside, at a place called the "Barquadier". The logs were formed into rafts and floated down the river, usually during the rainy season. The rafts were floated to a **"boom"** before reaching the mouth of the river. There they were squared for shipment to England.

Several different jobs were needed in this process. The huntsman's job was to search the forest to find the mahogany trees. Because this was an important skill, the huntsman was a very valued slave.

Old liquor bottles are very common finds. The Baymen were a drunken lot.

✐✐ *Bring a photograph of a mahogany tree. You can also find one in the Atlas of Belize. Observe the pictures and write a short description.*

✐✐ *Interview a sawmill or forestry worker and find out more about mahogany logging today.*

31

A "barbecue" was built at the base of the tree to help in the cutting.

The axemen cut down trees. This was a very dangerous and highly skilled job because the axe was heavy and sharp. The axemen had to stand on a springy platform called a "barbecue" about 12 or 15 feet high. The rest of the gang had to trim the tree after it had fallen. They also had to clear the path through which the logs were dragged.

It was the cattleman's job to take care of the cattle used to pull the huge trunks to the river. Women and children prepared the food and looked after the **provisions.**

It was stated in 1809 that "The gangs of negroes employed in this work consist of from ten to 50 each; few exceed the latter number. The large bodies are commonly divided into several small ones, a plan which it is supposed greatly facilitates labour". This was another major difference between the work experience of the slaves in Belize and those who worked in large gangs on the sugar plantations in the Caribbean. The smaller gangs reduced the need for close supervision. The foreman, whose job was chiefly to coordinate the gang's activities, had some authority. But the whip-wielding drivers of the sugar plantations were unknown in Belize.

The huge logs were carried to the river on carts pulled by cattle.

Other Work

Apart from the jobs that were directly connected with wood-cutting, slaves engaged in domestic work and some farming.

As elsewhere, the masters in Belize had slaves to clean their houses, sew, wash and iron their clothes, cook and serve food, and raise their children. Most of these domestics were women and children.

Slaves were often obligated to cultivate provisions, known as "making plantations". This allowed the master to save money by having the slaves grow their own food. Most of the slaves making plantations were women and old men. The young, strong men were used for the harder work of woodcutting. Many slaves also farmed on their own in their spare time.

There were other occupations among slaves, including sailors, blacksmiths, nurses and bakers. But most slaves had no choice and little freedom in their jobs. Young boys and girls started work waiting on their master's table, where they were taught to behave and obey their masters. Most of the young men joined the woodcutters, and the young women continued in domestic work. As they became older or sick, men were transferred to plantation work.

In Belize, a few settlers owned most of the slaves. In 1790, 20 estates owned over 100 slaves each, or more than half of the total. About a fifth of the settlers had no slaves. In the early 19th century the five largest owners owned 669 slaves, or over one quarter of the total.

Explain differences between slavery in the Caribbean and slavery in Belize. Explain the reasons for these differences.

Find out which of the foods we eat today come from Africa, which come from Europe, and which ones are native of the American continent.

Find out similarities and differences between African slaves and the Maya under British control. Did the British control both groups? How much control did they have over each group?

Slaves worked long hard hours in domestic jobs.

33

Master-Slave Relations

Superintendent Arthur reported in 1820 that many settlers treated their slaves with "extreme inhumanity" and "increasing severity and cruelty". In 1824, the settlement's chaplain stated that "there are instances, many instances, of horrible barbarity practiced there". There are descriptions in the Belize Archives of horrible cruelty to slaves. In Belize, the Superintendent, the head of the colonial administration, was in charge of the management of the slave system. Even if sometimes he and the settlers disagreed, they usually agreed on how to control the slaves. He would call the British navy for support when the slaves revolted. But the slaves were also controlled socially and **psychologically** by practicing the principle of "divide and rule".

Slaves were cruelly punished and sometimes killed by their masters.

Divide and Rule

The Colonial administration and the British settlers succeeded in dividing slaves from each other, African-born from Creole, blacks from brown, skilled and favoured from unskilled and unfavoured, converted Christians from "heathen", and so on. They also managed to divide the slaves from the "freed blacks and coloured" by giving the freemen just enough privileges and favours to make them identify with the whites.

The "free people of colour", as they were called, had some privileges but not as many as the white settlers had. They were free, but they could not hold commissions in the military. Their economic activities were restricted. They could not become judges or even sit on a jury. They had to own more property and live in the area longer than the whites in order to vote in elections. Many of the coloured people petitioned for more privileges. They stressed their loyalty and their "whiteness", and tried to keep separate from the black African slaves. By 1832 there were about 1,800 free coloured and black people in Belize (1,000 free coloured, 800 free black). This was almost half the total population.

The freemen of Belize were among the last in the British West Indies to receive equal rights with the white settlers. The white settlers controlled the early **legislative assembly** called the **Public Meeting**. In response to petitions, they allowed only one free coloured person at a time to become a member. They did not want the free people of colour to have power, but they expected the free coloureds to take their side against the blacks.

Once the free coloured in other British colonies in the Caribbean were accepted as equals, the Colonial Office in London pressed for change in Belize. The Office threatened to dissolve the Assembly if they did not agree. As a result, on July 5, 1831 the Public Meeting of Belize granted civil rights to "coloured Subjects of Free Condition".

The colonizers also succeeded in separating all the people of African ancestry from the Maya and Garifuna peoples, and the Maya and Garifuna from each other. In 1817 the magistrates of Belize were afraid that escaped slaves would join with the Maya and overpower the British. There is no recorded evidence that this ever happened, but it is believed that some runaway slaves were assisted by the Maya in their escape.

Slave Revolts

The Slaves' own actions tell us how they viewed slavery. They took drastic and dangerous actions, such as abortion, suicide, murder, desertion, and revolt to escape from slavery.

Slaves would risk
their lives to escape slavery.

Act out a situation in which the principle of "divide and rule" applies. You will find examples in the text.

Describe in your own words some of the privileges that "free men of colour" had.

The 1791
slave revolt in
St. Domingue brought
independence to Haiti.

There were four recorded revolts and many desertions of slaves in Belize. Three revolts took place during the period between 1760 and 1770. During this time the price of logwood fell. The settlers had a difficult time getting the provisions they needed to feed the slaves. Because they tried to export more logwood to make up for the lower price, the two thousand or more slaves in Belize had to work harder, but were fed less. They revolted in 1765, 1768, and 1773. The third revolt was the biggest. It began in May on the Belize River. Captain Davey arrived in St. George's Caye and reported in June:

"The Negroes before our people came up with them had taken five settlements and murdered six white men and were joined by several others the whole about fifty armed with sixteen Musquets, Cutlasses, etc. Our people attacked them on the 7th inst. but the Rebels after discharging their Pieces retired into the woods and it being late in the afternoon we could not pursue them". Unfortunately, there are no records giving the slaves' side of the story.

Fourteen rebels surrendered soon after, but Davey could not take the rest. The revolt continued through October. Davey reported that trade in the area had stopped, and that the white settlers were scared and "in a very bad situation". If they did not stop this revolt, they feared other slaves might run away or decide to revolt also.

The H.M.S. Garland was sent to Belize. Nineteen of the surviving escaped slaves were trying to reach the Spanish territories in the north. Captain Judd of the Garland sent some marines to stop them. Eleven of them, however, succeeded in reaching the Spanish port in the Rio Hondo and were not returned. These slaves had crossed about one hundred miles of bush in the five months since they began the revolt.

The last slave revolt in Belize took place in 1820 on the Belize and Sibun rivers. The Superintendent declared martial law because a "considerable number of slaves" were well armed. He sent troops up the river. He discovered that "the Negroes who had first deserted and had excited others to join them, had been treated with very unnecessary harshness by their owner, and had certainly good grounds for complaint".

Name four reasons why slaves tried to escape. Compare your answers with three other classmates. Make a new list.

Make a time line. Write on it all the events that took place between 1760 and 1773.

Imagine you are a slave in a British camp who wants to escape. Write a story plotting your escape.

Three Finger Jack, a famous maroon from the 18th century.

About ten days after the revolt began, Superintendent Arthur offered rewards for the apprehension of two black slaves, Will and Sharper, who were supposed to be the leaders. He offered "a free pardon to any of the other runaways, who will at this time voluntarily come in and deliver themselves". This revolt lasted for about one month.

Even when there was not a revolt the white settlers were scared that one would develop, so they kept what they called dangerous slaves away from the settlement. In 1791 the settlers were said to be "panic struck" when a French ship carrying over 200 rebels from Saint Domingue (Haiti) arrived. It was decided that "they should not be permitted to land so infectious a cargo". In 1796 the Belize Magistrates prohibited the landing of five Jamaican slaves who were suspected of having been **Maroons**, and in 1800 a Public Meeting discussed the settlers' "apprehension of internal convulsion and the horrors of Saint Domingo" happening in Belize.

Runaways

Apart from the four recorded revolts, we know the slaves were discontented because they ran away across the borders or created their own communities in the interior of Belize. It was relatively easy for the slaves to escape because they lived in small groups scattered in isolated parts of the country, and many slaves, like huntsmen, knew the bush well. In the 18th century, many slaves escaped north into Yucatan where the Spanish offered them freedom. Some of these former slaves even helped the Spaniards attack the British settlers in 1779.

The maroon village of Trelawney Town in Jamaica, lay deep in the forested hills.

When the Belize settlement expanded to the west and south early in the 19th century, the runaways went through the bush to the Peten in Guatemala, and by boat down the coast to Omoa and Trujillo in Honduras. In 1823, for example, masters complained that in a little over two months, 39 slaves had escaped to the Peten where there was a community of blacks who had left Belize. This happened over and over again.

Some of the runaways began independent communities within the Belize area. In 1816, such a community was reported "near Sibun River, very difficult to discover and guarded by poisonous snakes". The following year, Superintendent Arthur reported that "a considerable body of runaway slaves are formed in the interior." In 1820, he mentioned "two slave towns, which it appears have long been formed into the Blue Mountains to the Northward of Sibun." We cannot find the exact site of those towns now, but there is a tributary of the Sibun River called Runaway Creek. These communities provided a place to which other slaves could run.

This shows that slaves in Belize, like those elsewhere, rejected the system of slavery whenever they had the chance. They revolted, fought against their masters, ran away, and even killed themselves. But the slaves in Belize did not succeed in freeing themselves.

Indeed, the only known case in human history of a successful slave revolt is the one which began in Saint Domingue in 1791, and ended with the Declaration of Independence of the new nation of Haiti in 1804.

Look at the Atlas of Belize. Draw a map showing the geographical areas in which the runaway slaves settled.

Find out which country of the Caribbean was previously called St. Domingue. Locate this country on a map.

Toussaint l' Ouverture led the successful slave revolt in St. Domingue.

End of Slavery

Belize, like other British colonies, lasted as a slave society until 1838, when slaves were **emancipated** throughout the British empire.

Photograph of ex-slave

*Recorded by desire of William Usher
Bay of Honduras
Articles of Agreement between William Usher of the Bay of Honduras Gentleman of the one part and a free Negro Man named Tom formerly, but now named Thomas Usher of the other part. 1st. It is agreed and the said Thomas Usher hereby obliges himself faithfully, diligently and soberly to serve the said William Usher for two years, from and after the day of the date of these present, fully to be complete and ended, and that in all lawful work and business in which the said William Usher shall think proper to employ him. 2nd In consideration of such services, the said William Usher agrees and obliges himself during the said term of two years to furnish and provide the said Thomas Usher in good and sufficient meal, cloath and lodging becoming his station. In witness whereof the said parties to these presents have hereunto interchangeably set their hands, and seal, the eighth day of February in the year of our Lord, one thousand seven hundred and ninety.*

A 1790 agreement between a white baymen and a "free negro".

With the growth of **industrialization** in Great Britain came the need for a free market economy, where labourers were paid wages. By paying wages capitalists could make more profit by selling products to workers who now had their own money to spend. The slave system did not provide this.

Religious people and **humanitarians** had campaigned for the abolition of slavery since the 18th century. By 1831, increased humanitarian concern, the new economic interests in Britain, and slave revolts in the Caribbean combined to bring about the Act for the Abolition of Slavery. This was passed in Britain in June 1833.

The Abolition Act, however, did not produce drastic changes. Slavery was abolished, but land and labour were still controlled by Europeans. The Act included the introduction of the "apprenticeship" system, which was used to keep control over the workers and **condition** them to accept this control. Under this system, all slaves over the age of six years became "apprenticed labourers," and were forced to continue to work for their ex-masters without pay. This system lasted from 1834-1838 when it was abolished. The Abolition Act was generous and sympathetic to the slave owners but not to the slaves. The slave owners were even paid compensation by the British government for the loss of their slaves, but the slaves, even when they were legally free, still had to depend on their former owners for jobs, and were unable to own any land.

Until 1858 free land grants were given by the Superintendent but after 1858 the Colonial Secretary in Britain made it clear that Crown land would no longer be granted. He said that allowing the ex-slaves to obtain land might "discourage labour for wages".

The former masters in Belize controlled their ex-slaves by denying them land and by developing a system of labour laws, as we will see in Chapter 9. By these methods, the people of Belize, whether African, Maya or Garifuna, remained in a dependent situation, dominated by the British colonialists.

1824 Act to amend and consolidate the laws relating to the abolition of the slave trade.

What, in your opinion, contributed to the abolition of slavery? After slavery, what made ex-slaves still dependent on their ex-masters?

Part Two:
Dependent Belize in the World Economy

To understand our history, we must understand the place of Belize in the world **economy**. Over the last few hundred years more and more countries of the world have joined together in one global economic system. But the countries that make up this world economy are not equal. Those countries that began with more wealth and power were able to control and **exploit** poorer countries.

The Western European nations controlled the economies of their colonies – dominated their **capital**, land, labour and **markets**. As a result, the Western European countries benefited from the profits made in the colonies. They became richer while their colonies became poorer.

What were the disadvantages Belize had as a colony of Great Britain?

Why did Belize as a colony remain poor?

Belize was totally dependent on the changing demands of the European markets. Its development – or lack of it – was defined by the needs of Europeans. Although our land was rich in resources, our people stayed poor.

In Part Two we will find out how the market forces shifted forestry exploitation from logwood to mahogany and how the early settlers monopolized the land. We will also find out how development of an import trade led to the rise of a merchant class and the suppression of agriculture, although some people did engage in subsistence farming. Part Two also discusses the role of new immigrants – Garifuna, East Indians and Mestizos – in the expansion of the colonial economy.

An 18th century dye works. The logwood was ground into chips and boiled to extract the dye.

44

Chapter 6:
The Dominance of Forestry

The extraction of forest products in Belize created conditions different from British colonies in the Caribbean.

First, because forest work required less labour than sugar plantations, there was no need for a large population. This is why even today Belize has only 7 per cent of Jamaica's population, although we are twice the size of that island. Secondly, forest exploitation as practiced in Belize did not require much machinery, capital, or roads. Thirdly, there was no attempt to replace the trees that were cut. Eventually, slow-growing mahogany trees became scarce.

Logwood

We have already learned that the first product exported from Belize was logwood. But logwood did not remain the main economic activity in Belize. By 1770 there was more logwood in the market than was needed, and the price fell. Later, the development of cheaper man-made dyes in Europe lessened the need for logwood even more.

When settlers were driven out from Belize by the Spanish in 1779, they had already found an alternative that was more profitable and longer lasting – the export of mahogany.

Draw a map of Belize. Identify through drawing and labeling the natural resources. Refer to the Land and Sea Use and Economy maps of the Atlas of Belize.

Explain why logwood extraction declined. Why and when did mahogany exploitation start?

The exploitation of the forest was selective. Only mahogany trees were cut at first.

Mahogany

Mahogany dominated the economic, social and political life of our country until the middle of the 20th century.

In the 18th century, mahogany was valued in Europe by cabinet makers, by the shipbuilding industry, and later by builders of railroad carriages. The forests of Belize contained a great deal of mahogany. The British settlers were ready to log it.

The shift from logwood to mahogany cutting produced several dramatic changes in the settlement. The cutting of mahogany required more land, workers and capital and resulted in the creation of a small wealthy class who owned most of the land and labour.

Logs were squared before shipping.

Trade

Like logwood before it, mahogany suffered from rises and falls in demand and price. The years 1819 and 1826 were good years for mahogany, 1903 was bad. From 1834 to 1844 mahogany trading was very good but at the same time that exports were increasing, prices were going down. Between 1835 and 1841 the price dropped by half.

The rise in demand encouraged the cutting of trees, but no new trees were planted. Since mahogany takes many years to mature, the loggers had to move farther and farther inland to find trees. The time and effort increased the cost of logging. Since prices were going down at this time, the mahogany trade became less profitable.

The market continued to fluctuate. In the 1850's there was a severe decline in exports. By 1870, only two and three quarter million feet of mahogany were exported, the lowest yearly figure since the 1700's. By this time the settlers began to look for other economic activities.

A report of the Public Treasurer in 1860 noted that "agriculture is beginning to command a larger share of public attention". However, mahogany remained the most important export, and timber still earned the most money for the colony until 1959. It was only then that the combined value of sugar and citrus products was greater than the value of forestry products.

The total control of the economy by the logging companies meant the complete dependency of the colony on the mahogany trade. When the price of mahogany fell, it affected the whole economic and social life of Belize. At times, when companies went bankrupt their property was bought by other companies. This meant more land and capital ended up in the hands of a few.

Make a time line showing changes in the price of mahogany from 1903 until 1959. For every year given, write down what happened. What can you learn from this time line?

Explain the consequences of not planting new mahogany trees.

The forests of Belize were exploited for more than 200 years. It was done through methods that did not destroy much of the landscape. Discuss this with your class.

A United Fruit Co. banana plantation in the Stann Creek District.

The Merchant Class

Ever since the establishment of logwood settlements in Belize, The British settlers imported almost everything they needed to live and work. Most of what was needed but specially flour and salted pork, was imported.

The merchants and traders in Belize became rich and powerful. In 1885 the United States Consul in Belize wrote about "the tendency for persons to be disparaging about local agriculture efforts, lest success in the direction might reduce the profits from imported foodstuffs".

Which persons do you think would be the least interested in people producing more of their own food? Why?

At first, imports were totally controlled by the same people who controlled the export of timber. Then, in the 1920's, the **entrepot** trade with Central America grew and about four-fifths of the Central America trade went through Belize. Goods from Britain and the United States were imported into Belize first and then exported to other countries of the region. In 1860's, during the USA's **civil war**, the Belize merchants also profited by **contraband** trade with the Confederates.

Do you think the entrepot and contraband trades benefitted the majority of the population? Give your reasons.

Even without the entrepot and contraband trades the merchants were still very rich and powerful. They continued to be so long after forest exploitation declined.

Store of C. Biddle at which store views of Belize can be purchased

The Biddle's building
at North Front Street.

Chapter 7:
The Monopolization of Land

Land is a very important natural resource. The Maya, like Africans, believed that the land belonged to the entire community, not to individuals. But the Europeans believed land was private property that could be bought and sold at any time.

Land is a very important natural resource.

With colonization the European system of land ownership was brought to Belize. A small class of rich, **absentee landlords** developed. They took over the land for their own profit and excluded others from owning and often even from using the land. This system resulted in the growth of private wealth alongside wide-spread poverty while rich resources lay unused.

In Belize today there are about 200,000 people on almost 9,000 square miles of land. This means that there is a lot of land for very few people – one square mile of land for every 22 persons. Jamaica and Barbados have about 500 and 1,500 persons per square mile respectively.

So in Belize, a land scarcity is only possible if people are excluded from the ownership of land. This is what we find throughout our history.

✍✍ *Divide into two groups. One group is to discuss African and Maya beliefs on land ownership. The other group is to discuss the European view. Present each view to the class and talk on how they differ.*

✍✍ *What does "monopolization of land" mean to you. Write a story saying how land monopolization could affect the families in your community.*

Effects of the Monopolization of Land

During the years of slavery, about 12 families owned almost all of the private land in the settlement. Very little land was put into productive use. After the abolition of slavery, most of the population still could not own land. A few farmers tried to make a living on small farms without any real guarantees that the land was theirs.

The few landowners were more interested in the profits from logging than farming. People were not encouraged to farm and so remained dependent on imports. The most important effect of the **monopolization** of land was that the power to make decisions depended on ownership of land since only those who had land could vote. Land owners would also decide whether or not to use the land, and so controlled the amount of people working and their wages.

We will now look at how the early settlers monopolized the land.

Logwood and Mahogany "Works"

For more than a century the early British settlers had no **regulations** about ownership of land, and each person cut logwood wherever he found it. This lack of regulations was because Spain still held sovereignty over the territory. But in 1763, Britain signed the Treaty of Paris with Spain and gained the rights for its settlers to cut logwood. Then the settlers agreed on a system for regulating the boundaries of their logwood "works".

On April 10, 1765, the **Public Meeting** agreed that "when a person finds a spot of logwood unoccupied, and builds his hut, that spot shall be deemed his property". They also limited the amount of land a person could claim to 2,000 yards on the river. No cutter was allowed to hold more than one "work" in any river or creek.

✏️ In which ways did the possession of land influence the power to make decisions? Write a short essay of why you think this might have been unfair.

✏️ Make a time line that shows the dates and events that occurred from 1765 to Superintendent Arthur's proclamation in 1817. Illustrate the time line with drawings, showing the main events.

A Spanish map showing the areas allocated to the British for the cutting of logwood.

50

View of the
Belize Harbour.

The war between England and Spain in 1779 interrupted the cutters' work. The Peace Treaty of Versailles in 1783 gave them rights to cut only logwood, so the settlers were unhappy with the limitations imposed by the Treaty.

At a Public Meeting on June 12, 1784, the settlers re-established the regulations they had in 1765. They declared that the original settlers were to be "reinstated in their respective possessions... and all other property whether derived by right of possession or through purchase". As we can see, mahogany works and plantations, as well as logwood works, were established before the war in 1779 when they had to leave the settlement. It also proves that some of the land was already being bought and sold as if the cutters actually had rights of ownership.

In 1786 the Convention of London extended the boundary southward to the Sibun River, and permitted the settlers to cut mahogany, but Spain still claimed sovereignty. The settlers did not respect the boundaries defined in the treaties. By 1799, they had gone as far south as Deep River; by 1806 they were as far as the Rio Grande. In 1814, there were settlers at the Moho River. They reached the present southern boundary of Belize, the Sarstoon River, by 1820.

Talk about why the settlers were unhappy with the restrictions imposed by the Treaty of Versailles. Find out the different instances in which British settlers violated Spanish sovereignty in the Settlement.

Locate in the Atlas of Belize the rivers that are mentioned in this page.

Write a dialogue about two settlers discussing the meanings of "right of possession" and "through purchase".

Location Laws

In July and August, 1787, the settlers passed new laws about the mahogany works. These resolutions were known as "location laws". They required that a person "locate" a piece of land and stake his claim. The occupied lands were called locations or works, but they were actually treated as **freehold property**, being sold and inherited like private property.

Unlike the logwood works, the mahogany works covered large areas of land, and each person was allowed up to two mahogany works on any river. The largest areas of land were reserved for the richest settlers, those owning at least "four able negro men slaves".

The Public Meetings were controlled by the few wealthy white landowners. They passed **resolutions** to suit their own interests. Within a few months after these resolutions were announced, Superintendent Despard reported to London that 12 of the "Old Baymen" held four-fifths of the available land under the treaties, or about 2,000 square miles.

"Crown Lands" Established

When Superintendent George Arthur came to Belize in 1814, he was surprised at the "monopoly on the part of the monied cutters". He asked the Secretary of State for the colonies to take away from these settlers the right to grant lands to themselves. Superintendent Arthur issued a **proclamation** on October 28, 1817 that no occupancy of land would be permitted except by written permission from the Superintendent. He also ordered those who claimed land to record it, explaining how they got it. This was an unsuccessful way to stop the monopoly of land ownership. The Commission he appointed to check the owners' claims to the land was made up of the same people who were the largest landowners. They insisted that the land was correctly theirs.

Although the Superintendent was not able to stop the monopoly of land ownership, he did succeed in giving "the Crown" (the British monarchy) the sole rights to all unclaimed land.

This was especially important for the lands south of the Sibun which were outside the treaty limits. Superintendent Arthur was able to keep this land from wealthy land owners. The effect of this was still visible in Belize until the 1960's when most of the Crown Lands were south of the Sibun River.

Col. George Arthur,
Superintendent of Belize
from 1814-1822.

Organize a debate team. One side is to represent the "Crown", the other side the "old Baymen's families". Debate the issue of taking away from settlers the right to grant lands to themselves.

Interview the officer at the local Land's Department office and find out how much "Crown Land" there is in your district. Try to share your findings with schools in other districts.

The British Honduras Almanack provided a profile of the colony.

During the 1850's Britain signed treaties with the United States and with countries in Central America to define Britain's role in the area. In 1859, the Anglo-Guatemalan Treaty was signed, admitting British sovereignty over Belize and agreeing to the boundaries as we know them today. In 1862 the settlement of Belize was declared a colony and was named "British Honduras".

During the period from 1858 to 1861, the Honduras Land Titles Acts were passed to allow land in Belize to be sold even if a legal title to it could not be proven. This encouraged people in Britain to buy land in Belize.

The law was written in England by a lawyer employed by the company that became the British Honduras Company. This company's name was changed to the Belize Estate and Produce Company (B.E.C.) in 1875. The B.E.C. so completely dominated our country that the history of Belize for the next hundred years was largely the history of that company. It owned one-fifth of Belize, half the private land in the country.

Explain how the B.E.C. manage to own one-fifth of the country.

The Right to Land

To us in Africa, land was always recognized as belonging to the community. Each individual within our society had a right to the use of the land, because otherwise he could not earn his living and one cannot have the right to life without some means of maintaining life. But the African's right to land was simply the right to use it; he had no other right to it, nor did it occur to him to try and claim one.

Tanzania's President Julius Nyerere

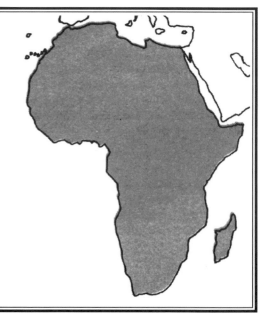

The Belize Estate and Produce Company

When the mahogany trade declined in the mid 1800's, many landowners went **bankrupt** and either sold their land to other owners, or sold it to the London merchants whom they owed large sums of money. **Partnerships** formed among some owners, and those with the most land and money were able to survive the depression. Eventually some partnerships grew to control huge amounts of land.

The largest of these partnerships was James Hyde & Co., a combination of two of the oldest settler families, James Hyde and James Bartlett, and John Hodge, a London merchant. They took advantage of all the land that was for sale during the depression, and also used marriages to control more. In 1859, James Hyde & Co. was bought out by the British Honduras Company, formed in England in 1859. In 1875 it changed its name to the Belize Estate and Produce Company (B.E.C.). With the land acquired from James Hyde & Co. and with other lands bought from bankrupt partnerships, the B.E.C. soon owned over a million acres in Belize, or about one-fifth of the entire country. This gave it enormous powers. Its lawyers drafted laws that helped them acquire more land.

In 1867, Maya villages on B.E.C. lands in the Yalbac Hills were destroyed by armed force and again in the 1930s fields and villages at Indian Church, San Jose and Yalbac were totally destroyed. The B.E.C. made hundreds homeless and fought strongly against the rights of its workers. Its chairmen were able to influence the Governor in Belize and the government in England. In 1847, the Chairman of the B.E.C. felt so confident about the company in Belize that he claimed "the interests of both are nearly identical".

Except for a brief period in the 1870's when it invested in sugar cultivation, the B.E.C.'s only use of the land was forestry exploitation. Yet it never used proper forest management nor did it replant trees – it just cut and shipped them. The B.E.C. was never able to use all its land, but it prevented others from using it in order to keep the population dependent on the Company and so better secure a cheap labour force.

The B.E.C.'s power in Belize lasted until the 1970's, when it was sold to an American company.

Chapter 8:
The Suppression of Agriculture

As we already know, there was always some agriculture in Belize. Some of the slaves cultivated provisions, either at the order of their masters to feed themselves or to sell. A number of free blacks and free coloured people also worked the land in small "provision grounds". The Garifuna, too, cultivated crops. In 1824, Punta Gorda was described as a town with 500 people who grew "cotton, rice, the cohune, banana, coconut, pineapple, orange, lemon, and plantain, with many other fruits". The Maya continued to live in the interior and cultivate the land.

But although these four groups practiced **subsistence farming** in the late 18th and 19th centuries, the land was largely used for logging. The landowners and woodcutters were generally opposed to agriculture, especially when people farmed on their own. In 1805, for example, they passed a resolution forbidding a slave "to hire himself out to himself with a view to pursue Trade".

Yet farming continued. It even increased significantly between 1817 and 1838. After 1818, disbanded soldiers from West Indian regiments and their families arrived in the settlement. Almost 700 people came, significantly increasing the population of only 4,000. Although many of them worked in the mahogany gangs, a large portion cultivated the land in small plots. But, like free coloured and blacks, they did not have the proper titles to their lands. Powerful landowners were often able to force them off their land so they had to work for someone else.

Discuss the difficulties that poorer people had in their attempts to practice agriculture.

Explain why the British did not want people to practice agriculture?

Imagine you are a subsistence farmer. List the products you will need to provide food and clothing for your family. Make a table showing which of these products you will be able to produce and which ones you will need to buy.

Land Denied

At the time slaves were emancipated in 1838, the British government sent an order to all the West Indian colonies, including Belize. All Crown grants of land would from then on be sold at a cost of 1 pound sterling per acre. This order was given at a time when many newly freed ex-slaves looked forward to getting their own land to farm. But this would not be so.

For almost 50 years, British settlers had taken large areas of land for free. Crown grants were officially issued free for 30 years. But as soon as slaves were freed, the Colonial Office in London added a fee. The effect of giving free grants of land, it said, "was to create indolent habits, to discourage labour for wages, and to leave large tracts of territory in a wild and unimproved state". It worried them that now, large numbers of black men and women would qualify for the free land grants and a scarcity of labour would develop.

Once again it was important to discourage the ex-slaves from working their own land in order to force them to work in the mahogany gangs. As a result of the new order of charging money for land, from 1838 to 1855 no Crown lands were sold and even by 1868 very little land had been sold.

The Garifuna

The early Caribs migrated to the Caribbean islands from South America. They were farmers, trappers and fishermen, and they made pottery and tools out of wood, stone and bone. They moved every few years, using dugout canoes to get from island to island. The Caribs were good warriors, and used many different kinds of weapons like bows and arrows, spears and clubs.

During the 17th century, Africans who had escaped from slavery intermarried with the Caribs who lived in the Windward Islands in the Eastern Caribbean. The new people which resulted are today called the Garifuna.

Sketch a map of the Caribbean. Draw a key for the map. Using arrows, trace a route showing where the Caribs came from. Show some of the island colonies from which slaves would try to run away. On the same map use arrows of different colours to trace the Garifuna's voluntary and forced migrations from their native land in St. Vincent.

Write a short story describing the experiences of a group of runaway slaves trying to reach the island of St. Vincent

Garifuna
Settlement Day.

58

The Garifuna strongly resisted European control. They kept the tradition of the earlier Caribs who fought against the Spanish invaders. The Caribs continued to fight against the British and the French, but the Europeans had guns and were eventually able to overpower them. One of their great leaders was Joseph Chatoyer. The British confined the Garifuna to the islands of St. Vincent and Dominica but they continued to fight until they were finally defeated in 1796. The following year the British forced about 5,000 Garifuna to move to the Bay Islands off the coast of Honduras. From there they migrated to the coastal areas of Nicaragua, Honduras, Guatemala, and southern Belize.

By 1802 there were 150 Garifuna settlers in Stann Creek. They fished and grew ground foods. In 1811 they were already taking their produce to Belize Town to sell. A Magistrates' Meeting in that year directed that all "Caribs" arriving at the Fort (in Belize Town) must get a permit or ticket from the Superintendent, or leave the Settlement within 48 hours. In 1814, it was reported that they tried to become a part of the Public Meeting, but were not allowed. In 1832, many Garifuna left Honduras after a civil war there. On 19 November 1832 they landed in Belize, led by Alejo Beni. To commemorate their arrival, we now celebrate this day as Garifuna Settlement Day, a national holiday.

The Baymen were afraid that the Garifuna would help slaves to escape. The Baymen therefore set out to build up a distrust and fear in the slaves against the Garifuna. They spread **propaganda** branding them as "devil worshippers" and "baby eaters". This created a prejudice that persisted for a long time.

Joseph Chatoyer led a revolt against the British in 1795.

View of the
Belize Town Market.

Garifuna drummer.

A view of
Stann Creek
in 1911.

The British colonialists and woodcutters saw the Garifuna as another source of labour for their mahogany camps. By 1833, many of them were working in the camps. The Public Meeting appointed a policeman in Stann Creek to deal with what they called the "runaway Caribs".

In 1855, the "Laws in Force Act" gave legal title to any person who was in "quiet and undisturbed possession of land" since 1840 – but this did not apply to the Garifuna on their lands. In 1857, the Crown Surveyor issued a notice to the Garifuna of Stann Creek stating that they must apply for a lease or they would lose their land and any buildings on them. They were treated as **squatters** on Crown lands. Later, the Crown Lands Ordinance of 1872 established "Carib Reserves" and "Maya Reserves". This prevented the Garifuna and Maya from owning land as their private property.

The colonial authorities continued to give preference to the large land owners, usually British, over the Garifuna, Maya and Africans. For example, in 1868, Governor Langden stated that small plantations, though occupied for over 50 years, could be "sold over the heads of the present occupiers to large proprietors".

Immigrants from India

Many of the sugar growers in the Caribbean needed more labour on their plantations and they re-introduced the system of "indentured labour". Under this system a person was encouraged to come to the Caribbean to work for a "master" for a certain number of years. After that he was free to work as he pleased. But too often circumstances forced him to "re-indenture" themselves, and agree to work for a further number of years.

Most of the indentured workers came from India. Under British colonialism thousands of people in India had become unemployed. Many were starving because of droughts and increased food prices. Between 1844 and 1917, 41,600 East Indians were indentured to work in the British colonies in the Caribbean.

The exact number of indentured labourers brought to Belize is not known. However, the numbers were never large. The census of 1891 lists only 291 persons living in the colony who were born in India. East Indians were put to work in the sugar estates in the Toledo and Corozal districts. Their descendants can still be found in areas such as Calcutta in the Corozal District and Forest Home in the Toledo District.

The British were never very respectful to East Indians, but they came from a very advanced civilization. They built magnificent cities and were great traders. Europeans had traded with India since ancient times. East Indians were advanced in mathematics, the languages, and the arts.

Forestry Still Dominant

The cultivation and export of sugar did not last long during this period. The late 19th century was a bad time to produce sugar and the plantations soon closed down. The small farms and milpas were more adaptable and continued their cultivation. But other attempts at **commercial** agriculture were not successful.

East Indian descendants from Calcutta Village.

✍✍ *Try to find out more about "Maya" and "Carib" reserves in Belize.*

✍✍ *Using the Atlas of Belize, identify Calcutta village. After which place is this village named? Find it on a world map.*

✍✍ *When did sugar cane farming become the main economic activity in the colony? Find out in which parts of Belize sugar cane grows best. Why is this so?*

Harvesting cacao.

Remains of
a sugar mill near
Sittee River.

✎ Explain the reasons why commercial agriculture in Belize was unsuccessful.

The sugar plantations that had spread to Toledo were closed down by the end of the century. An 1882 report by a man named Daniel Morris travelling in the south of the colony mentions fruit companies growing bananas, coconuts, cacao, and a factory for making cohune oil. By 1885, many of these estates in southern Belize had been abandoned. The export of bananas, first recorded in 1880, reached its peak in 1890, and soon disappeared.

Forestry, therefore, continued to be the most important economic activity and the big mahogany companies continued to hold the most power in Belize.

Commercial Agriculture

Some landowners did try to develop commercial agriculture in Belize, but were not successful. The British-Spanish treaties had not allowed it. In addition, the British discouraged the export of produce from Belize by making the taxes on crops from Belize higher than in other colonies. This made products from Belize more expensive which meant fewer people bought them. The landowners and merchants found that agriculture was not profitable. In the middle of the 19th century, however, events occurred which affected the population of Belize and had immediate effects on agriculture.

The Mestizo and the Maya

In 1848 the Maya of Yucatan in Mexico, revolted against the control over their land and the unjust social conditions. This revolt is known as the Caste War of Yucatan. Many thousands of Maya and Mestizos, people of mixed Spanish and Maya descent, fled to Belize.

After the war many of the **refugees** returned to Yucatan, but a large number stayed in Belize, mostly in the north. An official report in 1856 estimated the total population for Belize at 20,000. Over one-quarter of the people lived in the northern district, and most of these were refugees from the Yucatan. At that time, the population of Belize Town was about 7,000. Corozal Town had 4,500 people. San Estevan, with 1,300 Yucatecos, was the next largest town in the north.

A number of villages – San Pedro, Punta Consejo, Orange Walk, and San Antonio – had 200 or more persons each, mostly from Yucatan.

The Maya and Mestizo refugees who came were mostly small farmers. They continued this activity in Belize. The mahogany trade was declining and large areas of land, which had no more mahogany trees, were available. The big landowners were now willing to rent to these farmers.

By 1857 the new **immigrants** were growing large amounts of sugar, rice, corn and vegetables. In addition to growing enough sugar for Belize, they were able to export sugar and rum to Britain that year.

Once these new settlers showed that sugar could be successfully grown and exported, big landowners also began to grow cane. By 1868, over 3,000 acres of land were used for growing cane. One thousand and thirty-three tons were exported. Ten estates had steam machinery and four of these estates belonged to the British Honduras Company. By this time the British Honduras Company had become the biggest sugar producer in Belize.

Mestizos brought
their traditions
to Belize.

What was the greatest contribution of the Mestizo refugees to the economy of the colony in the latter part of the 19th century?

The Mestizo have also enriched Belizean culture. Divide into groups and gather information and material for a class presentation on the different aspects of Mestizo culture such as: oral tradition, music, food, etc.

Yucatecan immigrants
were fervent Catholics.

Old sugar mill
in the Corozal District.

Chapter 9:
How Colonialism Underdeveloped Belize

Colonialism created a pattern of **underdevelopment** in Belize. This pattern of relying only on forestry instead of developing the land created poverty and hardship for the workers and their families.

In the early 20th century, the forest industry revived for a short time. Mahogany and a new product, chicle, became the main export items. The United States began to import chicle, a gum taken from the sapodilla tree, to make chewing gum.

The chiclero cuts the trunk of the sapodilla tree to extract the chicle.

From 1929 until 1940 the economy of the United States collapsed. We call this the **Great Depression**. This caused the price of timber to fall. Later on, with the development of a chemical substitute for chicle, forestry declined again. Belize still did not have a good road system, loggers had to go farther and farther to find unused forests, and forestry continued to be managed badly. The Belize Estate and Produce Company started the first sawmill in Belize in 1933, but forestry still declined. Even as late as the 1950's foresters had not learned to care for the land and **manage** the industry by replanting the forests.

The gum is cooked over a fire, in big iron pots, and then poured into molds.

Chicle bleeding is a sustainable industry. Find out the meaning of this statement.

Residence of the Turton family, the biggest chicle contractor in the colony.

Sawmill workers.

✐✐ *All of the industries during colonial times, were based in the exportation of raw materials. How did this affect the economy? Make a list of raw materials and processed goods that are exported today.*

✐ *Write a short essay about some of the positive and negative aspects of the sale of land.*

All this time, however, mahogany remained the major export. Cedar and chicle were the next most important. Together these forest products made up 97 per cent of the forest production and 82 per cent of the total exports in 1935. Production costs continued to get higher, but the demand was low and prices went down.

The mahogany workers suffered the most. For example, in 1913 and 1914, 1,717 workers were paid an average of $12.64 a month. In the next season, 1914-15, only 714 workers were hired, at an average monthly wage of $8.21. Employment was insecure and seasonal. When mahogany was in demand and the prices were high more people were hired. When the industry was doing badly, the workers were paid less or lost their jobs. After the Great Depression, the forest industry never recovered.

Land

The mahogany landowners kept their power over the land until the middle of the 20th century. From 1859 the B.E.C. owned half of the best private land in Belize while a handful of others owned most of the other half. At the end of World War II, the distribution of land was almost the same as it had been at the end of the 19th century.

After the war many of the landowners sold their lands to the owners of other large estates. Most of these new owners were from the United States of America. Instead of using the land, they sold it again at a profit.

Even though the land was being bought and sold ownership remained in the hands of a few. A study as late as 1971 showed that 3 per cent of the landowners held 95 per cent of the land, and 91 per cent of the landowners held only 1 per cent in small plots. This study also showed that over 90 per cent of the freehold land in the country was owned by foreigners, and most of the land was not being used.

Agriculture

There were some attempts at commercial agriculture in the early 20th century. All failed in the period before World War II.

Since 1883, bananas were exported in small but increasing amounts. In 1911 the industry looked so promising that the United Fruit Company from the United States of America bought the Middlesex Estate in the Stann Creek District. A railway from the valley to a pier near Dangriga was built for the transportation of bananas. But plant disease, poor production methods and **marketing** problems were major obstacles to the success of the project. By the 1930's production stopped.

The Krammer Estates grew coffee and cacao. Tropical Oil Products experimented with cohune. There was also an Empire Starch Products Company. None of them survived for very long.

The railway was inaugurated in 1913 and dismantled twenty-four years later.

The colonial government started small land settlements in the 1930's. This was mostly to relieve the **unemployment** in Belize Town. Settlers were given poor lands, no secure land titles, and no help with producing or marketing their crops. After the 1931 hurricane, $200,000 of Hurricane Loan money was set aside for agricultural settlement, but in reality less than $70,000 was spent on agriculture. Instead most of the money was used to help the B.E.C.

Divide into groups. Do some research and devise a plan for the establishment of a new industry suitable to the conditions in your area. The presentation can include the name of the industry, production plan and an advertising campaign, TV commercial, jingle or poster, to help sell the product.

Belizean farmers are better off today than in colonial times. Discuss this statement.

Exporting bananas.

67

Make a list of factors that can help make agriculture successful.

How has improvement in infrastructure, such as roads and ports, helped Belizeans?

Use the Atlas of Belize. Note the main highways and ports in the country. Make a simple chart and list the main agricultural products of Belize; state where they are harvested and the means of transport employed to deliver them to the local and international markets.

Apart from the small citrus industry in Stann Creek, and the small sugar industry in Corozal, the only cultivation was the subsistence farming of Maya, Garifuna, East Indian, and a few Creole farmers. This was done on small plots and most of the farmers had to work in other occupations to earn extra money.

Agriculture could not succeed without **infrastructure** for transporting or marketing the produce. But the colonial government had built few roads or other means of transportation. The government was not interested in developing agriculture and did not help farmers learn more about how to cultivate and expand their plots. Because of these circumstances, the suppression of agriculture continued into the 20th century.

Society

When the economy does not improve, other aspects of life – social, political, cultural and educational – do not improve.

Belize was a society divided by race and class. Racism developed in Belize when the first Africans were brought here as slaves. We saw in Chapter 6 how the colonialists used the principle of divide and rule to keep the different peoples of Belize apart.

Crowds in their best clothes walk beside the race track on race day.

People were also divided by their religion, by where they lived, by occupation, by colour and by class. Divisions between people also occurred because communications were bad throughout the colony. It was very difficult to travel from one place to another and there was little contact between cultures or ways of life. Each group was encouraged to hate and fear the others, to feel as if they were better than every other group. They were taught to respect and identify with white leaders, the merchants and landowners who controlled the economy.

Dories were a common form of transport.

Those who accepted these ideas were rewarded. They could get better jobs, invitations to the Government House, or mentions on the King's Honours List. A **civil service** job would often get them noticed and provide these benefits.

Education was not a high priority for the colonial administration. In any case, British and later United States missionaries had already stepped in to run primary and secondary schools throughout the colony. The educational system, however, remained colonial. Students were taught how to be good British subjects. They learned more about Britain and Europe than about the Caribbean or the Americas, and even less about their own country Belize. They were encouraged to memorize facts rather than think for themselves.

Colonial education.

Lack of opportunities also created divisions. The economy was based on mahogany export and most men became mahogany workers. The people were not encouraged to farm or start their own businesses. The best paid jobs were held by the white and light-skinned Creole **elite.**

In this stagnant and unjust society, the small farmer, the worker and the unemployed were those who suffered most. And it was this **working class** who challenged and eventually changed the system.

✎ *There are yet many colonial attitudes that Belizeans should get rid of. Do you think Belizeans still behave and think this way? Explain your answer.*

✎✎ *Why did the colonial system of education focus on Europe and not on the Americas? Ask your parents or grandparents to teach you a song of colonial times that they learn in school. Sing it with your class.*

Part Three
Toward an Independent Belize

DURING THE 1930'S AND 1940'S workers' movements in the Caribbean began
to challenge the colonial system. World War II (1939-1945) brought many
changes and made it possible for many countries to become independent. In
1947 India won its independence from Britain. In 1945, Vietnam had declared
its independence from France, but the French opposed this move and launched
a bloody war which ended in a Vietnamese victory in 1954. Many African and

Asian nations also fought wars against colonialism. In the Caribbean and Belize there was no need to fight a war to gain independence.

After War World II the states on the winning side of the war organized the United Nations "to save succeeding generations from the scourge of war".

🖋 From what you have read, why do some countries take advantage of other countries?

🖋 Find out the meaning of "nationalism" and "decolonization".

🖋 Observe the picture below. Write a paragraph narrating its historical meaning.

In 1960, the United Nations General Assembly passed a resolution calling for the end of colonization. As more colonies became independent, they joined the U.N. and worked for decolonization everywhere. Even after independence, colonial countries still exercised a lot of control, since merchants and foreign companies controlled most of the wealth of these new nations.

Part Three will show that in spite of the resistance of the colonizers, gradually things started to change. We will see how workers organized and fought for their rights, how the nationalist movement joined forces with the workers to defeat colonialism. We will also find out why Belize's independence was delayed, and how it was finally achieved.

Chapter 10:
Workers' Resistance

In the early days of the settlement of Belize, the relationship between the foreign settlers and the Maya was clear. The Maya were independent forest dwellers, engaged in agriculture, hunting and trade, far removed from the influence of the British. Conflict arose when the British first tried to force the Maya to work for them, and later brought African slaves. Slaves, and later workers, attempted to gain more control over their lives and improve the conditions under which they worked. The employers were often unconcerned with the welfare of their employees, and cared more about their own profits. Throughout the history of Belize, workers and employers have often been in conflict.

In this chapter we will discuss how the working class in Belize resisted the unfair wages and the unfair labour laws.

We have seen how very few people were able to own land and how most people were forced to work for the foresters. Wages were kept very low. In 1836, the mahogany workers were paid between $12 to $15 per month, plus rations – seven quarts of flour and four pounds of pork a week. A century later the wages were still the same. Through the "advance system" the employer paid the worker some of his wages before he started working. The worker signed a **contract** by which he agreed to work for a certain period of time, often nine to eleven months. The contracting was done in Belize Town before Christmas. The workers used their advance money to spend Christmas with their families, then returned to the mahogany camps.

Once at the camps the labourer had to pay back the advance he was given. If he needed extra goods he had to buy them from his employer at high prices. The book-keeper **debited** his account for the costs. He also charged the worker fines if he was late to work, sick or absent or for being "lazy" or disrespectful to the supervisor. When a labourer finished his work for the season he would usually owe his employer

Write about the different ways people fought against colonialism.

Why do you think workers and employers have conflicts?

After the abolition of slavery, the workers of Belize were subjected to unfair labour laws and wages. Was the situation worse or better than during slavery?

Would you like to work under the contract described here? Discuss the charging of fines in relation to "being sick", "lazy" or "disrespectful".

money. He would then have to sign a contract for another year. All these injustices made the mahogany workers dependent and poor.

These were some of the ways the workers were controlled. Since the majority of the workers in Belize were scattered around the country in isolated mahogany camps, it was difficult for them to unite and revolt against the unfair practices. In the camps they also had to worry about their families who were left behind, and the consequences of a revolt.

British troops were relied upon to protect Britain's economic interests.

Labour Laws

The "Masters and Servants" laws of 1852 and 1885 were very harsh. It imposed a penalty of three months in jail with hard labour for anyone who did not work according to his contract. The employer was allowed to take any worker back by force if he left the work site for any reason. Workers were fined or sentenced to prison for up to three months for missing a day of work, for leaving a job unfinished, or for disobeying an employer or a supervisor. Any person who encouraged a worker to break the agreement with the employer could be sent to prison for three months. Most of the laws continued until the 1940's.

Read about the "Masters and Servants" laws. Say why you think the law was unfair. Try to write new laws that would be more fair to the workers.

The contract and labour laws were enforced by District Magistrates. In 1869, for example, the Magistrate at Corozal reported that all of the 26 cases decided by him under the labour laws consisted of discipline imposed on the workers, mostly for "absenting themselves from work without leave". Not a single decision was made in favour of the workers.

Describe a riot. Have you seen a riot in real life or film? Share it with your class.

Working Class Riots

Belizean workers still found ways to rebel against the difficult conditions under which they lived. Sometimes they protested violently. In late 1894 when the mahogany workers returned to Belize Town from the camps, they felt the effects of a **currency devaluation**. This devaluation had already caused a revolt by the Jamaican policemen who were stationed in Belize. Workers found that their pay worth even less – about half as much. They could not even afford the food they needed.

Under the leadership of John Alexander Tom, a group of workers went to see the Governor. The employers would not raise their salaries and the Governor said nothing could be done. The assembled workers rioted when they heard this announcement. They broke store windows and **looted**. Troops from a British warship stationed in the harbour landed and protected the merchants. Most of the leaders fled to Mexico because they realized they would not get a fair trial in Belize. The import houses and the mahogany companies were forced to increase wages to prevent more riots.

In 1919, when black Belizean servicemen returned from fighting in Europe during World War I, they rioted to protest the unequal, racist treatment they had received while fighting a war for the British. They destroyed many businesses owned by white merchants, and demanded that "British Honduras should be a Black man's country". Again British troops were brought in to stop the riots.

An important leader of the 1919 riot was Samuel Haynes. He became a follower of Marcus Garvey, the Jamaican-born black nationalist leader who formed the Universal Negro Improvement Association (UNIA) in Jamaica and the United States. Haynes also wrote the words of a song, "Land of the Gods" that later became Belize's national anthem, "Land of the Free".

Divide into groups and find out about the causes of World War I. Present and discuss the information with the class. Talk about what can be done to prevent war. Find out about the wars being fought in the world today. Talk about ways they could be stopped.

Why do you think the name of Belize's National Anthem was changed to "Land of the Free"?

While in Europe, Belizean servicemen faced discrimination.

The introduction of the tractor caused unemployment.

A brief economic boom created by World War I provided a few more jobs in the forest industry. But in 1914 food prices were rising, and after the war ended in 1918 unemployment increased again. In the mid 1920's the invention of the tractor made it easier to haul logs. The mahogany work season was cut from eleven to six months and fewer workers were needed.

The Great Depression

In 1929, a major economic crisis started in North America, Europe and other industrialized countries of the world. It had far-reaching effects in Belize as well. In the industrialized countries millions of people lost their jobs and country after country restricted the importation of foreign goods.

Belize felt the effects of the Great Depression. Export prices were reduced, imports dropped sharply and government finances collapsed. Unemployment increased. In 1931, a major hurricane added physical destruction to the social and economic problems.

Discuss the advantages and disadvantages of the introduction of the tractor in the forest industry. Make two drawings to show how logging changed.

Divide into groups. Talk to people old enough to remember the difficult economic times during the Great Depression. Share your findings with the class.

The colonial government sponsored work programmes, but they were temporary and only provided limited relief. Throughout Belize, people suffered extreme poverty and near starvation, especially in Belize City. Rice lab, a porridge consisting of boiled rice with sugar, was distributed to the public at the gates of the Belize City prison to keep the people from starving.

Thousands of people died in the 1931 hurricane

In February 1934, a group who called themselves the "Unemployed Brigade" organized a march through the streets of Belize City to the office of the Governor demanding work. He replied by asking all the unemployed to register. When nearly 1,800 did, he offered jobs to only 80 persons, breaking stones at 25 cents a day on the northern road. The leaders of the Unemployed Brigade became discouraged and resigned in an **open letter** to the governor.

Soberanis and the Labour Movement

Antonio Soberanis, one of the demonstrators, felt that the brigade should not simply give up. He declared that he would prefer to be "a dead hero than a living coward". He began to hold regular meetings at the Battlefield, now Battlefield Park in Belize City, demanding work for the unemployed. He also attacked the B.E.C., the rich merchants, the colonial officials, and the colonial system for not helping the people. By July he had formed the Labour and Unemployed Association (LUA). In September, he organized **pickets** and **boycotts** against some of the most important merchant houses. In late September he travelled to Dangriga where he succeeded in raising the wages of dock workers loading grapefruit from 8 cents to 25 cents an hour.

Antonio Soberanis, 1897-1975

Soberanis and Pettie's Snakes

Soberanis' arrest after the October 1934 riot caused a great uproar. When it was learned that he had been refused bail, a crowd of 2,000 assembled outside the police station. Christopher Velasquez, called "Pettie", the town's snake man, had an idea about how to free Soberanis. He would clear the station by letting two of his snakes loose, then Soberanis could escape.

He put his "wowla" and his "tommygoff" on the veranda of the Police Station and was reported to have said "Do your work; go get Tony." A great cheer went up from the crowd.

The desired effect, however, was not achieved. Major Mathews beat one of the snakes with his baton and drove them off. Velasquez was later charged with obstructing the police, and was sentenced to six months hard labour. Soberanis remained in jail for a month.

Belize City during colonial times.

Back in Belize City, Soberanis organized a picket of the B.E.C. sawmill to convince its workers to **strike** for more pay. On October 1, 1934 the picket turned into a riot. A demonstrator was shot in the neck. The sawmill and several business places were closed down by the rioters. The Acting Governor promised the demonstrators $3,000 for immediate "outdoor relief", then imprisoned 17 of the demonstrators. When Soberanis went to post bail for the demonstrators, he himself was arrested. He was not granted **bail** for over a month. One of the leaders of the riot was later sentenced to three years hard labour.

During the five weeks that Soberanis spent in jail, a split developed in the movement. Many of the other leaders left LUA. Soberanis recruited new officers. In April 1935 he urged road workers in Dangriga to strike for more wages. This almost started another riot.

The colonial administration passed three new laws in 1935 which allowed the police to ban processions, gave the Governor powers in the event of an emergency, and did not allow criticism of the government. These laws were used against Soberanis in October 1935, when he addressed a crowd in Corozal Town. He condemned the Belize merchants as "bloodsuckers", and called the Governor and the King "crooks". This led to his arrest, and on his appearance before a sympathetic judge, to a fine of only 25 dollars.

Find out about other people that believe in social justice as Antonio Soberanis did? Share your findings with the class.

In the history of Belize do you find people who fought for freedom? Were they all fighting in the same way? Make posters of these people with a description of the cause they fought for.

Antonio Soberanis with Black Cross nurses in the 1950's

After the split in the leadership, Soberanis' movement was not very strong. The two sides wasted their energy talking against each other. But although this movement was short-lived, it gave Soberanis the opportunity to confront the important social and economic problems of the day.

He attacked the colonial officials and questioned the need for Crown colony government. Most importantly, Soberanis took the movement out into the districts, so that the entire country began to think about the rights of all workers.

True Belizean Heroes

Through the years, the British colonial governments defined our heroes and patriots for us.

For example, the Bayman Thomas Paslow is honoured because he fought bravely at the Battle of St. George's Caye to defend his property. But that does not make him a Belizean patriot. He treated his own slaves so badly that his fellow Baymen had to bring him to trial for his inhumanity.

Heroes who have been loyal to the people of Belize have been ignored in our history, but they helped make the country what it is today. **Will** *and* **Sharper** *led the slave revolt of 1820.* **Charles Freeman** *gave up his own freedom trying to help Belizean slaves achieve theirs.* **John Alexander Tom** *led the labourers in their demands of 1894. Nurses* **Vivian Seay** *and* **Cleopatra White** *of the Black Cross Nurses who dedicated their lives to community service, and* **Gwendolyn Lizarraga**, *successful political leader whose work to improve housing and education in Belize is remembered by many.*

There are many other heroes in Belize, and you can discover them for yourselves.

The Paslow building.

Philip Goldson
International Airport.

Chapter 11:
The Nationalist Movement

The struggle of the workers led by Soberanis played an important part in the birth of the nationalist movement in Belize. People began to question what colonialism had done for Belize. They began to wonder why a country with so many resources, with such wealthy landowners and merchants, had so many poor people. The poor economic and social conditions in the 1950's also helped them begin to think about self-government and independence.

Economic and Social Conditions

During the 1930's and 1940's the economy was still based on forestry, but this industry was declining continuously. During World War II (1939-1945) the industry had revived for a while. Unemployment had also been eased because thousands of workers **emigrated** to Britain for forestry jobs, to Panama to work in building the Canal and to the southern United States to work in agricultural estates. But after the war they came home to unemployment and poverty.

A local legislator stated in 1949 that "the privations suffered during the Depression were but bagatelles compared to the sufferings the people are undergoing now". He warned that people might be forced by their misery and hunger to resort to crime and rioting.

The working class suffered from unemployment, low wages, bad housing, severe malnutrition, and poor health care. In early 1950, a British reporter complained that "the Colony has always been run exclusively for what could be got out of it . . . of the 35,000 employable from a total population of 60,000, 8,000 or nearly a quarter are without work or working part-time, earning less than twelve shillings per week. Belize City, with its 22,000 people, is about the most shockingly depressed spot in the whole British/West Indies – perhaps in the Commonwealth. Hunger, poverty, the filthy conditions under which the people live are incredible."

What led Belizeans to think about self-government and independence?

What were some of the economic and social ills that affected the working class?

Find out the causes of World War II. Discuss them with the class. Do you think a World War III is possible? What could cause it?

Make a pie chart showing the percentage of people unemployed or working only part-time in 1950. Do you think the situation was much worse for women trying to find a job? Discuss this with your classmates.

The devaluation of the Belize dollar, on December 31, 1949, resulted in the immediate worsening of the workers' situation.

Campaign Against Colonialism

✎ Make a list of some of the objectives of the People's United Party.

✎✎ Imagine you are one of the leaders of the PUP. You are going to visit the village of Bermudian Landing. Write a speech that will convince the people of what you believe in.

✎✎ Find out what role the B.E.C. played in the colony. Report your findings to your teacher.

The People's Committee was formed the very night the Belize dollar was devalued. What started as a protest against devaluation became a general assault against the entire colonial system. On September 29, 1950 the People's Committee became the People's United Party (PUP). Its objective was "to gain for the people of this country political independence and economic independence". After a split in 1951, the main leaders of the party were Leigh Richardson, George Price and Philip Goldson.

One of the first political tasks set by these leaders was to create a national unity out of the divisions created by colonialism. They travelled throughout the country calling on the people to unite and fight for their rights and for a say in running their country. They educated the people about the problems of colonialism. They explained how poverty and misery were caused by the system of exploitation, and the special role the B.E.C. played in this process.

George Price, leader of the
People's United Party.

These young leaders were not only concerned with raising the living standards of the people, but they were also determined to make a complete break with the colonial past. In a memorial to the King from the People's Committee in February 1950, they declared that the social evils under which Belizeans were suffering "are caused by colonial exploitation that takes abroad the wealth of the country and leaves it impoverished and destitute. There is in us a growing and determined aspiration to eventual self-government."

Alliance with Workers

From the time of the People's Committee, a strong alliance was formed with the working class movement. The working class was represented by the General Workers Union (GWU). By 1951, the leaders of the PUP and the GWU were almost the same.

In October 1952 they called a national strike to protest against the economic conditions which had steadily worsened since devaluation. Even occasional rises in wages made little difference because prices kept increasing. The B.E.C. was a major target of the strike, but government workers went on strike too, as well as workers of the United Fruit Company and several other companies. The strike was called off after ten days when the government and the other companies – except the B.E.C. – agreed to negotiate with the union for better wages and working conditions.

The B.E.C. held out for 49 days and stopped the strike by using **scab labour** protected by police. In spite of this, the leaders felt that the strike was a success. It had shown that working class **solidarity** gave the workers power and won them benefits. This established the PUP in the public mind as a party for working people. The membership in the GWU increased quickly to over 8,000.

The Constitutional Struggle

Although the PUP emphasized change in the economic conditions, their main effort was to challenge the colonial political system. They demanded political power for the people, and

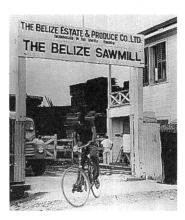

Belize Estate & Produce Co. Sawmill.

Why do you think the working class accepted the PUP's ideals?

Imagine you are a worker. You know that if you go on strike your family will suffer. Write a letter to them so they understand you.

83

this required **constitutional** change. First the people had to be given the right to vote.

✐ *In which way was universal adult suffrage important?*

✐✐ *Interview 20 people who are going to be 18 years soon. Find out if they have registered for voting. Make a graph with the results of the survey.*

✐✐ *You are a member of a middle class family. Write a letter to a friend explaining why you believe in colonialism.*

In the fight for **universal adult suffrage**, the right for all adults to vote, the nationalist leaders tried to change people's attitudes. Many people, especially those from the **middle class**, argued that the colony was too underdeveloped, its people too backward and **illiterate**, to have the right to vote. Instead they suggested three options: a literacy test; a system of indirect voting by the districts outside of Belize City; and reserve powers for the governor.

In a report on constitutional change published in 1951, the middle class praised what they called the tradition of "British Institutions, British laws, and those high principles of fair play, freedom and justice which are characteristic of the Anglo-Saxon". They argued that the colonial system had created a fair administration, under which every resident could "retain for his own use the fruit of his labours". Most workers, however, did not agree.

The PUP attacked the recommendations made in the report. The argument that the country must be developed before colonialism could be abolished ignored the important fact that colonialism was the cause of underdevelopment. In order for the country to develop, its people had to be free. Leigh Richardson explained in 1952:

"But those who argue that social, economic and educational development must take place first, before political indepen-

A segment of Belizean society identified with the colonial system.

84

dence, are putting the cart before the horse. On the contrary, political independence is the first essential step forward, in order that a government may be established, representative of the people and not subservient to the exploiting monopolist interest. Only then does the possibility exist to utilize the resources of the country for independent social and economic development, instead of for tribute to absentee shareholders."

There were some people in Belize who felt threatened by any changes from the colonial system. These were the "loyalists". They comprised mostly those who benefitted from the colonial system - traders, civil servants, and some professionals. They were the "middle class" who felt that their opposition to the nationalist movement was their patriotic duty.

The PUP, with the strong support of the people, won universal adult suffrage in 1954. In elections held that year it won eight of the nine elected seats and 67 per cent of the vote. In the following years, Belizeans went on to win increased participation through new constitutions. In 1964, ten years after adult suffrage, Belizeans gained self-government.

Forward to nationhood.

85

Belize Legislative History to 1981

Date	Body	Official	Nominated	Elected	Total	Majority	Comments
		Members					
1854-1870	Legislative Assembly	3	0	18	21	Elected	Power of Public Meeting gradually reduced in first half of 19th Century. After 1848 influx of refugees from Yucatan, English settlers push for formal British sovereignty. Britain signs treaty with U.S.A. about British presence in Central America, and asserts sovereignty over Belize.
1871-1889	Legislative Council	6	4	0	10	Official	Maya attacks on the settlement lead British settlers to call for more direct rule from Britain. British colonial policy was then in favour of more direct rule throughout the West Indies.
1890-1891	Legislative Council	5	4	0	9	Official	Local elite not satisfied with '71 Legislative Council, win fight for majority of nominated members. In 1890, request for elected members refused on ground that of about 30,000 inhabitants only 400 were of European descent.
1892-1912	Legislative Council	4	5	0	9	Unofficial	
1913-1935	Legislative Council	6	7	0	13	Unofficial	
1936-1938	Legislative Council	6	2	5	13	Unofficial	Elected representation being granted in West Indies; changing local elite want more power. Voter and candidate qualifications remains about the same as in 1854. Governor has "reserve powers". In 1945 there were 822 registered voters in a population of 63,390.
1939-1945	Legislative Council	6	2	6	14	Unofficial	
1945-1954	Legislative Council	4	4	6	14	Unofficial	
1954-1960	Legislative Assembly	3	3	9	15	Elected	Nationalist movement wins universal adult suffrage, and more elected members in the legislature.
1960-1963	Legislative Assembly	2	5	18	25	Elected	Struggle for self-determination in 50's and 60's leads to more elected members and eventually to limited self-government.
1864-1981 (a) House of Representatives (b) Senate	National Assembly	0 / 0	0 / 8	18 / 0	18 / 8	Elected / Nominated	Constitution for limited self-government is meant to lead to independence and last only a short time; British colonies in the Caribbean are becoming independent. Cabinet Government instituted.

The Political Struggle

It was a long struggle of political and civil action that enabled the people to make gains in the 1950's. There was a lot of hard work involved in organizing the movement for decolonization. At times the struggle became violent. In 1950, a crowd stoned the homes of politicians regarded as pro-British, and knocked out the police guard at the Governor's residence. The government declared a state of emergency that lasted 137 days. Violent incidents also occurred during a national strike in 1952.

Generally, the threat of violence and the reality of thousands of people voicing their demands was enough to cause the authorities concern. They were forced to make **concessions**.

The colonial administrators created a new party financed by the B.E.C. They used force by declaring a state of emergency, passing laws, prosecuting and jailing leaders. They gave in to small reforms. They appealed to people's loyalty to the King.

How do you think one can become a "mental slave"? Share your thoughts with the class. Observe the picture below and name some colonial characteristics.

Divide into two groups to debate the pros and cons of independence versus colonialism..

Mental Slaves

Physical slaves often are a distinct liability to the owner. Mental slaves are slaves in the most profitable way, doing their master's bidding without hope of reward and without desire for fight and insurrection. This is the form of slavery that Britain maintained in her colonies...encouraging the inevitable bootlickers among their inhabitants to fasten among their fellow citizens a distinct feeling of inferiority and utter dependence on Britain, both of which feelings are then combined and presented in a compound called loyalty to Britain.

Leigh Richardson, 1950

George V, coronation day celebrations.

Chapter 12:
A Society Transformed

❧❧ *Find out what is the process by which a Belizean can get a piece of land or a house lot. Write it down. From what you learn, do you think there is a scarcity of land?*

❧❧ *Write an essay about why owning land is still important for most people.*

❧❧ *Having obtained an acre of land from government how would you use it to improve your economic situation?. Write a detailed plan of your project.*

Some important changes began to occur in Belize once colonialism was seriously challenged in the 1950's. This chapter explains some of the changes that make the Belize of today different from the Belize we described in Chapter 9.

Land Distribution

In 1962, a new law was passed to give people rights over the land they lived on. But it only required the landlord to give one year's notice to throw the farmers off the land. To give farmers more control over their land, the government had to use an older law, the 1947 Land Acquisition Ordinance. Under this law, the government could buy land from big landlords and redistribute it to the people. The government could also accept land from big landowners, like the B.E.C., in exchange for land taxes they owed. This made it possible for the government to distribute some 200,000 acres to Belizean farmers between 1971 and 1975. From 1975 to 1982, a further 325,000 acres were redistributed.

We have already seen that in 1971 many foreigners owned land in Belize and did not use it. But an important step towards preserving Belize's land was the passing of the Alien

---

Servants to New Masters

Our development and our growth shall not be by paths that would deprive us of the ownership and control of our assets and resources. We shall not attempt to enhance and increase our treasures by ways that would make us in the end second-class citizens or servants to new masters.

George Price

Landholding Ordinance in 1973. This law regulated the right of foreigners to buy land, and introduced certain development conditions. Foreigners had to get a license from the Minister after showing how they would develop the land. This law helped to reduce the number of foreigners who bought land to re-sell it for profit. But there were still changes to be made, because even after independence, most of the best agricultural land was owned by foreigners.

How does the Alien Land-holding Ordinance stop capitalists from having easy access to land?

Land Use

Perhaps the most important change in land use was the shift from an economy based on forestry to one based on agriculture. In the 1950's forestry finally became less important in Belize's economy. Forest products fell from 80 per cent of our export trade in the 1950's to only 1.9 per cent of our export trade in 1981. That year, the value of agricultural exports was $105.5 million, while the value of forestry exports was $2.6 million. Today, forestry's share of the export trade is 3.2 per cent.

Find out information about Belize's physical environment. Make a list of the problems that affect the environment. Make a list of things you can do to protect and preserve the environment.

Belize has about 5.7 million acres of land, but only 2.2 million acres are considered suitable for agricultural development. However, much of this land is not easy to reach. In 1981, 237,000 acres of land had permanent crops, and 20,000 acres of land were used for milpa farming.

Citrus production in the Stann Creek Valley.

Vegetable production.

Cattle ranching.

89

Draw a cartoon showing three positive and three negative aspects of tourism.

Find out the meaning of recycle. Make a collage using only recycled materials such as pieces of plastic, bottle covers, scrap wood, old newspapers etc...

Our forests are still a very important source of wealth to us, but we must be careful to conserve and use them properly. With the increase in tourism in the last few years, the preservation of our forests and marine resources is becoming more important. The creative use of the forest, in such ways as eco-tourism, herbal medicine and chicle production can provide many jobs without harming the environment.

Another important change has been the government's decision to set aside lands as protected areas, where the land is closely managed to avoid damage to the environment and our historical heritage. These protected areas provide homes for a wide variety of rare and endangered animals and plants. The protected areas include national parks, wildlife sanctuaries, forest, nature, marine and archaeological reserves.

Forest reserve.

Marine reserve.

Agriculture

Illustrate and name some of the most important species of Belize's flora and fauna.

There are two kinds of agriculture in Belize – export or estate agriculture, and small farming. The most important export crop is sugar. This industry began to grow after 1964 when the British **transnational** company, Tate and Lyle, took over the old Corozal sugar factory and later built a modern factory at Tower Hill in Orange Walk. As a result of demands by Belizean cane farmers in the 1960's, almost all of the 65,000 acres in cane today are now owned by the farmers themselves.

The second most important crop is citrus. This industry is centered in the Stann Creek Valley. In 1994, the total value of citrus exports was 35.1 million dollars. Several other agricultural products for export are encouraged, notably rice, bananas, and beef.

There have been important improvements in the conditions of the small farmer. Attempts have been made to help farmers with credit, markets, land preparation, roads and technical assistance. In all these areas, however, there is rarely enough help to meet the growing demand.

There is also need for better planning and administration. The small farmer has many disadvantages, mostly the result of the lack of an agricultural tradition.

Since the 1970's, the fishing industry also became important. Many years ago, fishery resources were controlled by foreigners who bought the products cheaply from our fishermen. In the 1970's, fishermen joined into powerful, well organized co-operatives. Fishing villages became prosperous. In addition, the income from exporting fish went directly to the fishermen. In 1994, the value of our fish exports was $26.4 million, mostly from lobster sales. The importance of some fishing **co-operatives** has since declined. Today many fishermen work in the tourism industry, and have become tourist guides, diving instructors and hotel workers.

Cane worker.

Discuss with your class why agriculture is so important for the country and its people. List the main products of Belize. Which of these are mainly for export, and which are mainly for local consumption?

Citrus production in the
Stann Creek Valley.

Northern Fishermen
Cooperative's, freezing plant.

Trade

Imported goods at sale in supermarket.

During the course of a week, bring to school containers and wrappings of food and other articles consumed in your house. Make a chart with the products that are imported and the ones produced locally. What can you learn from the chart?

In the early days of colonialism, the settlement was only allowed to trade with Britain, its "mother country". This continued as Britain became the leading industrial nation in the 19th century. The U.S.A. has since become our major trading partner.

Most of our exports go to the developed countries. This makes our economy very dependent on the economic conditions in these countries. Our major exports are agricultural products. the majority of these products go out as **raw material**s, or only partly processed or packaged. Our imported goods, however, are chiefly manufactured and processed items. The cost of **manufactured** goods is higher and prices increase frequently. Therefore, the price of our imports usually rise while the price of our exports often falls. Both the prices of raw materials and manufactured goods are set by industrial countries.

The result is a widening of the "trade gap" – meaning that more and more, the value of what we buy is greater than the value of what we sell. For example, in 1975, the value of exports was $129.7 million, while the value of imports was $185.5 million. The gap was $55.8 million. In 1981 all our exports earned $238 million while our imports cost $323.9 million - a difference of $85.9 million. In 1994, the trade gap was 226.6 millions.

Unless Belize can reduce its import costs and increase the value of its exports, this problem will continue. As an agricultural country with a small population, we can produce more

Cashew products from Crooked Tree.

San Ignacio street market.

of the food we need. In order for this situation to change, Belize has to spend less money on imports and concentrate on growing its own food.

There have been some attempts to diversify our trade. In 1971, Belize joined the Caribbean Free Trade Association, which in 1974 became the Caribbean Community (CARICOM). This is a trading bloc made up of 13 Commonwealth Caribbean countries with about five million people. By trading with each other we encourage development in each of our countries. We also lessen our dependence on only one or two industrial countries. Increasingly, even the developed countries are forming trade blocs to protect their trade. For example, in 1994, Canada, the United States of America and Mexico formed the North American Free Trade Association (NAFTA) to regulate trade.

Infrastructure

These economic changes would not have been possible without great improvements in what is known as the country's "infrastructure" – including services such as roads, communications, electricity, and water. The development of a road network throughout the country has been one of the most important changes. The Belize City deep-water port is also an important development. The expanded international airport, the small domestic airport, and the modern telephone system established in the 1970's all aid communications. In the 1960's, the increased distribution of electricity country-wide helped our economic growth and greatly improved the quality of life for thousands of Belizeans. Finally, the establishment of the new capital city of Belmopan in the Cayo District created a new infrastructure and marked a new direction by developing the interior of Belize.

✍✍ *Write a paragraph describing a farmer's market. Why do you think some people still prefer imported products to local products?*

✍✍ *Find out which countries are members of CARICOM. Locate them on a map. In which way does CARICOM help its members?*

✍ *Write a short story on how your life would be different without the infrastructure Belize has today.*

Road construction on the Hummingbird Highway

Bel-China bridge in Belize City.

Social Changes

The most dramatic change in Belizean society has been the growth in population. In 1931 there were just over 50,000 people in Belize. In 1946, the population was still less than 60,000. But by 1970, the population had doubled to just under 120,000. In 1980, it was over 145,000 and by the 1991 **census**, 200,000 people lived in Belize. There has also been a steady decrease in **urbanization** and an increase in the rural population.

Educational opportunities in British Honduras were limited to primary and secondary school. Very few people had an opportunity to attend university. The few who studied abroad would return and become part of the Civil Service or enter private business or professional careers.

Self-government brought marginal relief to the working classes but in the late 1960's and 1970's the PUP and the local middle class elite found themselves challenged by a more

Draw a graph showing the population growth of Belize. Discuss the graph with the class. Name some important factors that have contributed to the increase in population.

The Crowd Called UBAD

"Black and Proud"

UBAD spoke about global racism and urged the black people in Belize to learn their history and stand for their rights. Their fiery rethoric and unconventional attire, afro hairdos and dashikis, attracted a large following of urban youth, but earned only suspicion from the established middle-class and politicians.

Some of their leaders successfully defended themselves against criminal charges brought against them by the authorities. They never gained political power, but what they fought for – freedom, justice and equality– went to the core of the problems Belize was facing at the time.

UBAD's legacy to Belize is the AMANDALA weekly newspaper, one of the most widely read newspapers in the country today.

radical element of Belizean society - a younger, more educated, more vocal group of students who had returned from studies at universities in the US, the West Indies and the UK. This group was called UBAD (United Black Association for Development) PAC (People's Action Committee) and RAM (Revolitical Action Movement). The most prominent of these groups was UBAD, which was formed in 1969 as a movement for black nationalism, but evolved in the 1970's as a political party, the UBAD Party for Freedom, Justice and Equality.

Another major change has been the increasing involvement of the population in the political, economic and social life of Belize. In the past, the majority of the population had no say, and the rights of many were ignored. Today that is changing.

Educational opportunities are part of this change. Under colonialism, very little was invested in education. In 1930, only 3.3 per cent of the country's budget was for education; in 1951 it was still only 8 per cent. In the 1990's about 17 per cent of the budget is used for education. The number of primary schools has grown as well. Every district now has at least one secondary school, and most have Sixth Forms. The University College of Belize (UCB) has replaced the former Belize College of Arts, Science and Technology (BELCAST). Adult education centres are being created, and centres for employment training and vocational centres are now found throughout the country.

Get a copy of Amandala. Write a short essay talking about the social concerns expressed in the newspaper.

Which major social changes have gradually taken place since independence?

Find out what maternity benefits, sickness benefits and retirement benefits the Belize Social Security offers to the insured workers.

University College of Belize graduation ceremony.

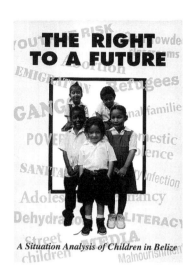

Some NGO's work to promote the
right of children to a better life.

Northern Fishermen Co-operative
was founded in 1960.

Important advances have also been made in other social services such as health and housing. Although the government has begun to provide low-cost housing, the need is still great, especially in Belize City. The social security system, which began in 1981, provides an important service for workers by insuring them against hardships.

Voluntary Associations

An important development that also helped to bring many changes is the increase in the organization of people in unions and other types of non-governmental organizations (NGOs). A major change was the growth of the trade union movement. By uniting, members acquired a strength which the individual worker could never have. With this power they negotiated with their employers and gained many benefits, such as better wages and working conditions. Forming trade unions also helped the workers to stop some of the injustices in the economic system.

NGOs, on the other hand, provide social and humanitarian services and help government with their responsibilities in these areas.

Another form of organization is the co-operative movement. Producers combine their knowledge and finances to develop their industry successfully. We have seen how co-operatives made development and prosperity possible for fishermen. Farmers also rely on their co-operatives for technical assistance and marketing.

The growth of the credit union movement has also helped to provide loans and services for those with little money. Today there are 23 active credit unions in Belize with a membership of about 30,000 and total savings of over $14 million. In addition, there are other types of people's organizations, such as the associations of sugar, citrus, grain, and livestock producers, tourism and businesses.

These organizations give people the opportunity to participate more fully in the economic, social, and political life of the country.

Looking Forward

Much has been accomplished since the 1950's. Throughout our history, there were many social divisions in Belize – today some of these divisions, along with economic differences, still keep many young people from the opportunities they have a right to. That many of our qualified people come from humble origins is a remarkable achievement.

Many colonial attitudes have changed, and since independence Belizeans have developed a new appreciation for their country and a better understanding of Belize's place in the modern world.

The beautiful Rio On pools in the Mountain Pine Ridge are a popular destination.

Talk on how much you know about Belize. Talk to your parents and grandparents. Find out how much they knew when they were your own age. How are things different?

During a visit to the Belize Zoo children enjoy learning about Belize's environment.

Learning about the Maya at Xunantunich.

97

Chapter 13:
Regional Influences on Belize

Although Belize was a British colony until September 21, 1981, the United States of America had a strong influence on Belize. Its influence was actually greater than that of Britain or any other country in the region.

In 1935, the British Governor of Belize, Sir Alan Burns, wrote:

"The whole colony is, however, largely influenced by the comparative proximity of the U.S. and the people as a whole are more American than British in their outlook. This may be due to a limited extent to the cinema, but is more directly attributable to the influence of the trade and education."

The U.S.'s interest and influence on Belize began well over a hundred years ago. In order to understand its growth, it is first necessary to study the expansion of U.S. influence throughout the region.

USA Influence

The United States of America won its independence in 1776 after a bloody war with Britain. Two generations later, it was well on its way to becoming the greatest power in the western hemisphere.

On December 2, 1823, U.S. President James Monroe made a speech to Congress which introduced its new foreign policy, the "Monroe Doctrine". In short, he told the European powers to keep their "hands off the Americas". The U.S. considered the Caribbean and Central America its back yard and wanted to control the countries and instill U.S. values in them. As U.S. influence expanded throughout the Americas, their businesses began to invest heavily in these countries.

In 1903 the U.S. supported an insurrection in Panama, which was then a part of Colombia. This resulted in the setting up of the independent state of Panama. A treaty was immediately

Look at the drawing on page 98. Describe the influences shown. Discuss the positive and negative influences in our culture. Make a list of other influences you know of.

Discuss with your class how the Monroe Doctrine protected the economic and political interests of the United States.

Divide into groups. Choose a country where the U.S.A. has intervened militarily. Explain the major reasons for the intervention. State whether you think the reasons for the interventions have been economic, political or humanitarian.

signed giving the U.S. the right to build a canal that connected the Atlantic Ocean to the Pacific. The Treaty also allowed the U.S. to rent the land from Panama in **perpetuity**.

From the early 1900s U.S. economic interests in the Americas increased significantly. U.S. investments rose from 17 per cent in 1914 to 40 per cent in 1929.

These investments were protected by U.S. military strength. Between 1898 and 1920, U.S. marines landed in the countries of the region more than 20 times. Before the military withdrew, the U.S. often protected their interests by leaving behind local military dictators, such as the Somozas in Nicaragua, and Rafael Trujillo in the Dominican Republic.

Read and explain in your own words the sentence "The whole hemisphere will be ours" Discuss it with your class.

The Whole Hemisphere Will Be Ours

Fate has written our policy...the trade of the world must and can be ours. And we shall get it... We will cover the ocean with our merchant marine. We will build a navy to the measure of our greatness. Great colonies, governing themselves, flying our flag, and trading with us, will grow about our ports of trade. Our institutions will follow... And American Law, American Order, American Civilization and the American flag will plant themselves on shores hitherto bloody...

U.S.A. Senator Beveridge, 1890

We do control the destinies of Central America and we do so for the simple reason that the national interest absolutely dictates such a course...Until now Central America has always understood that governments which we recognize and support stay in power, while those we do not recognize and support fall.

Excerpt from a 1927 State Department Memorandum by Under-Secretary of State, Robert Olds

The day is not far distant when three Stars and Stripes at three equidistant points will mark our territory: one at the North Pole, another at the Panama Canal, and the third at the South Pole. The whole hemisphere will be ours in fact as, by virtue of our superiority of race, it already is ours morally.

U.S.A. President William Howard Taft, 1912

The U.S. respected British sovereignty over Belize, and this protected Belize from the kinds of military, economic, and political interventions that took place in other parts of Central America. But because the U.S. is so close to Belize, its influence was inevitable.

In recent years, U.S involvement in the Americas, although highly economic, has been tempered toward more humanitarian concerns. In 1978, for example, President Jimmy Carter re-negotiated a new Panama Canal Treaty with the then President of Panama, General Omar Torrijos, which allowed Panama to regain full sovereignty over the canal zone.

U.S. Role in the Guatemalan Claim

When the U.S. and Britain signed the Clayton-Bulwer Treaty in 1850, they hoped to resolve some of their differences in Central America. Article 1 of the Treaty agreed that the two countries would not "fortify, or colonize, or assume, or exercise any dominion over Nicaragua, Costa Rica, the Mosquito Coast, or any part of Central America".

It was not clear whether the term "Central America" included Belize. Based on the treaty, in 1853 a new U.S. government tried to persuade Britain to withdraw from Central America and Belize. The frustrated British Foreign Secretary, Lord Palmerston, declared that "These Yankees are most astute bullies and are always trying to see how far they can go."

Draw a map of Central America. Identify the countries. Locate the Panama Canal and discuss its geographical importance.

Research and discuss the meanings of "third world" and "developing countries". Make a list of countries belonging to each category. Find similarities and differences among the countries in each list.

**Panama President
General Omar Torrijos
and U.S President
Jimmy Carter.**

In 1856 this dispute was finally resolved when Britain and the U.S. signed the Dallas-Clarendon Treaty. The "Mosquito Protectorate" and the Bay Islands, which were held by Britain, were to be part of Nicaragua and Honduras respectively. British Honduras was declared to be unaffected by the Clayton-Bulwer Treaty and Belize's southern border was recognized as the Sarstoon River. The hope was that the western limits with Guatemala would be fixed within two years. Three years later the Anglo-Guatemalan Treaty of 1859 was signed, and the dispute was temporarily settled.

Trade

Find out why chicle was important, why it failed and why it is presently reviving. Talk to any old person who remembers the time when chicle was important.

Say in which way quotas help the economy of Belize. Illustrate with examples.

Find out about Belize's deep water ports and why they are important.

Trade between Belize and the U.S. during the 1800s and 1900s was confined to the export of mahogany and chicle and the import of food and other supplies. But trade was not always legal, as Belize merchants became infamous for smuggling goods to the Confederates during the U.S. Civil War in the 1860's and for smuggling whisky to the U.S. during **prohibition** in the 1920's. by the 1930s the importance of U.S. trade rivaled that of the British.

By 1949, over 70 per cent of Belize's imports came from the U.S. Their share of Belize's exports also increased significantly in later years – from 12.4 per cent in 1961 to 33.5 per cent in 1965, largely as a result of the sugar **quota** granted by the U.S. to Belize. In 1981, 60.8 per cent of our exports went to the U.S., and 35.4 per cent of our imports came from that

The port of Big Creek in the Stann Creek District.

country. In 1994, we sold 53.1 per cent of our products to the U.S. and bought 41.5 per cent of our total imports from them.

Immigration and Emigration

In the 1860's, British settlers in Belize encouraged immigration from the U.S. Hundreds of Confederates came to Belize after the Civil War in search of land to develop. Few of the Confederates, however, stayed – most returned to the U.S. or moved on to Latin America. A group of Methodists from Mississippi did settle in the Toledo District in 1867 and established 12 sugar estates, but most were gone by 1910.

Emigration of Belizeans to the United States of America has been more consistent. During the Second World War, over 2,000 men migrated to the Panama Canal Zone to work for U.S. employers. In 1941 and the following years, thousands of workers went to work on farms in the southern United States. Since then, a steady flow of Belizeans have emigrated to the U.S. in search of work. About 60 per cent enter or stay in the country illegally. This emigration has had a number of important influences in Belize. Economically, the money the emigrants send home is an important source of income for their families. They have also brought U.S. culture to Belize. In recent years, some emigrants have returned to settle in Belize and are contributing to the development of the nation. Others who have been **deported** because of illegal activities in the United States have brought back some of the violence of U.S. society, and its negative consequences.

Name some of the reasons why many Belizeans migrate to the USA. Point out the positive aspects and the negative aspects of Belizean emigration to the USA. Start a debate on the two positions.

Interview some recent immigrants. Find out what attracted them to Belize. Make a list of the most common answers. Share the reasons with your class.

Write a letter to a relative living in the USA. In your letter convince him/her to return to Belize.

Many grandparents are left responsible for young children after their parents migrate to the U.S.

Every day several flights leave to the U.S. from the Philip Goldson International Airport.

Investment, Speculation and Influence

Make a pie chart showing how much of the total area of Belize was owned by U.S. citizens in 1970. Colour your chart.

In small groups, discuss how the media influences the way we live. The influences can be negative or positive.

St John's College, Loyola Park, Belize City.

Important United States investment in Belize dates back to at least 1911, when the United Fruit Company purchased the Middlesex Estate in Stann Creek Valley. They began large-scale operations on 12,500 acres of land. Although the estate was later abandoned due to plant disease, other U.S. companies have continued to invest in Belize over the years.

After the Second World War, many foreigners **speculated** in land in Belize. Hundreds of thousands of acres were bought by U.S. nationals. In 1980 even the B.E.C. was bought out by a company from the U.S. By independence, about 80 per cent of all privately owned land, or about 40 per cent of all land in Belize, was owned by U.S. citizens. Government lands, most of which are leased to Belizeans, made up the rest.

Other aspects of U.S. influence include education and culture. Over the years, missionaries from the U.S. have established schools in partnership with the Government. In the 1930's they were said to be responsible for the education of more than half the total population. A major contribution to this influence was the presence of Roman Catholic Jesuit priests from the United States who ran primary schools throughout the country. The Jesuits established a secondary school, Saint John's College in 1887. This school played a prominent role in the rise of an educated class which later led the challenge to the colonial system. The cultural influence of the U.S. is also felt through the **media**: television, newspapers, magazines, and radio.

Mexico, Central America and the Caribbean

All these influences – economic, social, cultural, and educational – have resulted in a strongly-felt U.S. presence in every aspect of the country's life. But as far back as 1950, George Price wrote that Belize's "economy and way of life are **interdependent** with the U.S.A. and with Central America".

Before colonialism, the people who lived in what is now Belize were linked socially and commercially with Mexico, Guatemala, northern Honduras and El Salvador. These connections grew weaker because of British and North American interests and disputes with Guatemala. Now that Belize is independent and its disputes are for the most part resolved, these links are again growing stronger.

The Caste War of Yucatan in 1847 brought many Mexican refugees into Belize. The war also brought to the forefront the need to define Belize's northern boundary with Mexico. The boundary was finally agreed upon in 1893, but the treaty between Britain and Mexico was not finalized until 1897. At one time, Mexico expressed interest in claiming a portion of northern Belize if Guatemala gained Belizean territory. Yet Mexico has strongly supported Belize's independence since 1977, when it voted in favour of a pro-Belize resolution at the United Nations. Since independence, the two countries have formed a strong bond of friendship through social, commercial and educational agreements that have helped our country greatly.

Our relations with Central American countries were slow to form because of continued border disputes with the Government of Guatemala. During the 1970s, civil wars in Central America forced many people to leave their countries in search of a safer environment. Many came to Belize and settled mostly in the rural areas. The new immigrants have gradually integrated into Belizean society and have contributed to the development of the country. With more immigration from the area and less tension with Guatemala, a closer relationship has developed.

Belize's northern border.

In what ways do you think Belize benefits from its ties with Mexico and Central America? List the ways in which the arrival of Central American immigrants have benefitted Belize.

Imagine you are going to Mexico for a visit. You would like to tell your new friend there about Belize. Try to communicate in different ways: gestures, language, drawings etc...

Mexico's Institute of Cooperation and Culture in Belize City.

In which way is the society and economy of Belize similar to those of other Caribbean countries.

Listen to Bob Marley. Pay attention to the words in the songs. Try to find out about his life and what he believed in.

Belize's relations with the English-speaking Caribbean date back to the British conquest of Jamaica in 1655. The British conducted the defense and administration of the settlement of Belize from their base in Jamaica. Slaves and colonial administrators were imported from Jamaica and other British colonies in the Caribbean, and the laws of Jamaica were enforced in the settlement.

Belize's experience with colonialism was similar to the Caribbean's. Because of this we share many social, cultural, economic and political similarities. The newly independent Caribbean countries were the leaders in supporting Belizean independence and our **diplomatic** resistance to the Guatemalan claim to our territory. Our membership in the Caribbean Free Trade Association (CARIFTA) and later the Caribbean Community (CARICOM) was the first time we participated in international organizations. Since independence, Belize has worked closely with Caribbean countries in regional integration efforts.

Caribbean Heads of Government meeting in Belize.

Chapter 14:
Belize on the World Stage

Since its birth in 1950, the goal of the Belize nationalist movement was self-government and independence. Within a few years the spirit of nationalism had taken root. People from all over the country considered themselves to be citizens of one nation. In 1961, after self-government, the British government agreed that Belize could become constitutionally independent within a short time. By that time colonialism was on the retreat throughout the world.

In 1960 the United Nations passed a historic resolution fully supporting independence for colonial territories and peoples. Many countries were emerging from colonialism to independence, some after years of armed struggle. In the Caribbean, Jamaica and Trinidad and Tobago became independent in 1962. It was time for Belize to become independent also.

The only reason Belize had to wait more than 20 years before achieving independence was because the government of Guatemala insisted on a land claim to Belize. Guatemala threatened to use force against Belize if it became independent without first settling the claim. Because of the need to find support for these issues, Belize was involved on the world stage even before it became independent.

Talk about the main reason why Belize's independence was delayed.

Find out instances of the United Nations working toward World Peace. Make a list with all the facts. Bring newspaper clippings to put in your bulletin board.

Find out about countries that are in conflict today due to land disputes. Identify the countries on a world map.

Belize at the U.N.

The Guatemalan Claim

When the Latin American countries became independent from Spain in 1821, they established the rule that the boundaries of these new republics would be the same as when the territories were ruled by Spain. Guatemala claimed that Belize had been part of the Spanish territory. However, the British argued that they had been in control of the area before 1821, and so this rule did not apply to Belize.

At the core of Guatemala's claim to Belizean territory is the Anglo-Guatemalan Treaty of 1859. From the British point of view, the agreement simply declared the boundaries of an area Britain already ruled. Those boundaries still exist today. From the Guatemalan point of view, which was developed after the agreement was signed, it was a treaty of **cession**, by which Guatemala gave up right to the land. For the treaty to take effect, Britain had to help build a road to improve communications between Guatemala and the Atlantic coast. Because this road was never built, Guatemala insisted that the treaty was broken. In 1945, a new Guatemalan constitution declared Belize a part of Guatemala, and the country threatened to invade. Guatemala threatened similar action throughout Belize's recent history, such as in 1972, 1975 and 1977. Each time an increased British military presence prevented the invasions.

Negotiations

Until 1962, the elected representatives of Belize had no say in the negotiations concerning Guatemala's claim to Belizean territory. Since then, the history of these negotiations can be divided into three parts: the secretive period, the break-out period, and the post-independence period.

During the secretive period from 1962 to 1975, negotiations were carried out behind closed doors. Little information was given to the people of Belize or of the world. The Belizeans were observers in the British team.

The U.S. stayed out of the dispute, expressing its desire for the countries to arrive at a settlement through negotiations.

Many maps of Guatemala included Belize.

A few days before independence Guatemala closed its consulate in Belize City.

108

But in the 1960's, former Guatemalan President Ydigoras Fuentes claimed that while he was President in 1961, the U.S. had agreed to support Guatemala in return for using Guatemalan territory as a base for the invasion of Cuba.

In 1965, Guatemala, Britain and Belize agreed to ask U.S. President Lyndon Johnson to **mediate** the dispute. The proposals presented by the mediator Bethuel Webster three years later would have given Guatemala a large amount of control over the affairs of Belize. The Belize government totally rejected them.

In 1975, after 13 years of secret and fruitless negotiations, the government of Guatemala demanded that Belize give up all the land south of the Monkey River as a way of settling the dispute. The Belize government decided it was time to create a new strategy. This break-out period occurred from 1975 to 1981. Belizeans took the issue to the international community and won their support.

It was believed that international support would strengthen Belize's position, force Britain to support Belize's insistence on keeping its territory intact, win the backing of Latin American countries, and gain the support of the U.S.

Draw a time-line illustrating the negotiations to settle the Guatemalan claim between 1962 and 1981.

Prepare a brief summary of why Guatemala claimed Belize. Find out what you can about the present situation in respect to the Belize-Guatemala dispute.

On a physical map of Belize, look up and trace the piece of land that Guatemala claimed in 1975 in order to settle its dispute with Belize.

Belizeans rejected the Webster proposals.

109

Look for articles in newspapers and books that talk about Belize's struggle for independence. You may copy an excerpt or paragraph and read it to the class.

Considering that its members are of very different political social and economic systems, discuss why the NAM is successful in its policies.

What role did the Non-Aligned Movement play in Belize's struggle for independence?

Most countries did not know enough about the controversy and so supported Guatemala's claim. Because Belize was not independent it had no diplomatic relations with any country. However, Belize's close relations with several CARICOM countries helped its representatives attend Commonwealth meetings and United Nations sessions. Belizeans were able to **lobby** for support. Of greatest importance was the support Belize received from the Non-Aligned Movement (NAM).

Lobbying around the world

The Non-Aligned Movement was formed in 1961 to offer an alternative of peace and co-operation while the world was dividing into two blocs: one on the side of the United States of America and Western Europe, and the other on the side of the Union of Soviet Socialist Republics (USSR) and Eastern Europe.

Meeting of the Non-Aligned Movement.

The Movement was open to states of very different political, economic and social systems. A major concern of the Non-Aligned countries was to support all peoples struggling for their independence and liberation.

By 1983, the Movement had 101 member countries. Since the end of the **cold war** in the 1990's, the Movement now concentrates mainly on helping development in Third World countries.

In August 1975, Belize won the Movement's full support for secure independence and **territorial integrity**.

It was very difficult to get the Latin American countries to understand and support Belize's position. In 1975 at the U.N. the only Spanish-speaking Latin American country that supported Belize was Cuba. In 1976, the President of Panama, Omar Torrijos, was persuaded to support our cause. He actively campaigned among other Latin American countries. Mexico, Venezuela, Argentina and Peru joined the support in 1977. In 1979, the Sandinista revolution of Nicaragua overthrew the Somoza dictatorship, Guatemala's most committed ally. The new government declared its full support for Belize.

From 1975 to 1979, the U.S. **abstained** on all the United Nations resolutions concerning Belize's independence, sovereignty and territorial integrity. Finally, in 1980, it changed its policy of **neutrality** and voted in favour of the U.N. resolution that called for the independence of Belize. This resolution was adopted in November 1980. It demanded the secure independence of Belize, with all its territory, before the next session of the U.N. in 1981. It called on Britain to continue to defend Belize, and on all countries to come to its assistance. One hundred and thirty-nine countries voted in favour of the resolution, with seven abstentions and none against. Guatemala refused to vote.

That same year, the Organization of American States (OAS) fully endorsed the U.N. resolution. This was an important victory, because until then the OAS had supported Guatemala.

Which Latin American countries eventually supported Belize's move towards independence?

What role did the Organization of America States (OAS) play for the achievement of independence?

Research and share your findings with regards to the following: What role did George Price play in the struggle for independence?

**George Price
addressing the United Nations.**

Continued Negotiations

The next problem was achieving independence with territorial integrity and security. It was important to keep Britain's full support since their military presence after independence was vital. Belize also had to satisfy its new important ally, the U.S.A. We had to prove that we were doing everything possible to find a negotiated settlement to the dispute. And we had to convince the government of Guatemala to accept a peaceful solution without expecting us to give up land or give up control over our land.

The hope was to negotiate a solution before becoming independent. Guatemala needed to find a way to drop its claim. In February 1981, Guatemala made serious efforts to reach agreement by dropping its demand for mainland cession which it had insisted on for many years. But agreement could still not be reached because Belize refused to agree to anything that would not give us full sovereignty and territorial integrity.

On March 11, 1981, Britain, Guatemala and Belize signed "The Heads of Agreement". This document stated that there was no final agreement nor even specific proposals, but rather

The Belize Defence Force was created in 1978.

Harrier planes were relied upon to defend Belize against a possible Guatemala aggression.

areas for discussion that would form the basis for a final agreement after negotiations. Guatemala agreed to recognize an independent Belize within its existing borders, but only if agreement could be reached on other points in the document. These other points included the "use and enjoyment" of certain cayes, free port facilities, freedom of transit on two roads, facilitation of oil pipelines, co-operation in security, and a non-aggression pact. These were not spelled out specifically. It was left for future negotiators of the three countries to hammer out the details and reach a final agreement acceptable to all sides. The Heads of Agreement was interpreted by some sections of the Belizean population as unacceptable concessions given to Guatemala. The result was wide-spread disquiet, uncertainty and civil action including rioting in Belize City and setting fire to a government office. This agreement lapsed before independence.

Violence is reported in the press during the Heads of Agreement riots in Belize City.

The Road to Independence

A long history of resistance to oppression characterizes the road leading to September 21. The colonialism suffered by Belize and other Caribbean countries was all the more effective because it was so subtle, instilling in the colonized people a sense of inferiority and dependence, promoting disunity among the people and providing a justification of itself that many of the colonized accepted as true.

In such circumstances it is difficult to sustain an organized and conscious anti-colonial struggle. Our history shows, however, that somehow, despite all the difficulties, an unbroken thread of resistance has been maintained.

The victory of independence belongs to each and every Belizean through this history who, in no matter how a small a way, demonstrated by his action his conviction that nothing is more abhorrent than slavery in any form, and nothing is more precious than freedom and independence.

The struggle continues.

Independence Booklet, September 1981, Government of Belize.

Independence

In our international campaign and in negotiations, Belize insisted that the right of the people to independence was a separate issue from the negotiations to end the Guatemalan claim. We insisted that independence must be achieved by 1981 even if negotiations were not successful. If necessary, negotiations would continue after independence.

Which two factors ensured the security of Belize as an independent country?

The negotiation failed, but Belize went on to independence, assisted in our security by the continued British military presence and by our membership in the United Nations.

On September 21, 1981, Belize became an independent nation. In every town and in many villages throughout the country, a midnight flag-raising ceremony was held. The new flag of Belize was raised to the strains of the Belizean anthem.

Independence Day celebrations, 21st September 1981.

114

We have seen how, unlike most countries, Belize entered actively on the world stage while it was still a colony. Indeed, its entry on the world stage was a necessary and crucial part of the struggle for independence. But Belize could not be a full member of the international organizations while we were still a colony. Now that Belize is independent, it has all the rights of a sovereign state in the international arena.

On September 25, 1981, Belize was admitted as a member of the United Nations. On the same day it became a full member of the Non-Aligned Movement, after being a member with "special status" since 1976. On Independence Day Belize was also admitted to membership of the Commonwealth of Nations.

Today, Belize plays its full role as a member of the Organization of American States and other international social, political and economic organizations. As an independent state, Belize has gained the respect of most of the nations of the world, including Guatemala. Although the Guatemalan claim has not yet been completely resolved, Guatemala recognized Belize's independence in 1991, and the two countries have finally established full diplomatic relations.

Belize at the Organization of American States.

Central American Heads of Government Conference, Belize City.

🖊 *Explain how Belize's initiative on the world stage helped independence.*

🖊🖊 *Prepare an interview with five questions. Interview two persons and find out how they felt about independence. Share the interview with your class.*

Prime Minister Hon. Said Musa.

Our System of Government

Belize is a monarchical state but is governed by a system of representative parliamentary democracy roughly patterned after a British parliament. The Head of State is Queen Elizabeth II, who is Queen of Belize as well as being Queen of the United Kingdom and a number of former British colonies. The Queen is represented in Belize by a Governor-General who is a citizen of Belize. The National Assembly is bi-cameral, comprising the House of Representatives and the Senate. Municipal and local councils are elective in all areas of the country.

Persons who are eighteen years or older vote in elections for the candidates of their choice. The political party which gains the largest number of seats in a general election forms the Government, those with lesser numbers are in the Opposition. Together, the Government and the Opposition form the 29-seat House of Representatives, which debates and passes the laws of the country.

There is also a Senate of eight persons who are appointed by the Governor-General on the advice of the Prime Minister and the Leader of the Opposition. They review the laws passed by the House of Representatives and ratify them. The Senate's power is limited. They can delay laws passed by the House of Representatives, but cannot reject them.

✎ *Draw a diagram showing the structure of Government.*

✎✎ *Find out the names of the Prime Minister and his cabinet of ministers with their respective portfolios.*

Election campaign propaganda.

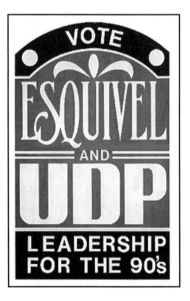

The newspaper with the greatest circulation in Belize

AMANDALA BELIZE

(36 PAGES) .85c

NO. 1344

BELIZE CITY, FRIDAY, JUNE 16, 1995

Millions changed hands in the kingdom of the blind. Is Ephriam the one-eyed man?

**Cabinet blames Usher:
Usher fingers Goldson:
Barrow insists Usher!**

A free press openly
discusses public issues.

The Governor General appoints as Prime Minister, the person who is leader of the political party with the largest number of seats. This Prime Minister presides over a Cabinet of ministers, who are mostly elected politicians. This Cabinet is responsible for all policy decisions. Government decisions are implemented by a bureaucracy, which is the Public Service.

Representative democracy thrives vigorously in Belize. Since independence, there has been a change of government in every general election between 1984 and 1993. the two main political parties, the People's United Party (PUP) and the United Democratic Party (UDP), have both formed governments. Smaller third parties have emerged from time to time, but have not successfully challenged either of the main parties.

This climate of political freedom, public opinion and a free press actively influence government decisions, and safeguard the independence and sovereignty that Belizeans have won for themselves.

In your opinion, have the citizens of Belize enjoyed real democracy? Why? Why not?

Divide the class into groups. Decide on any current issue of interest. One group is to argue in favour, the other against. After hearing the two perspectives, take a secret vote.

Through history we have blamed colonialism for our problems. Now that we are responsible for our own affairs we have nobody to blame but ourselves. Debate this statement.

Cultural Freedom

Culture gives a nation its identity. The way people adjust to their environment, the things they create and do, are part of our culture. A people's culture includes what is passed on from generation to generation; but culture is also constantly being created by people.

Belize's culture while rich is still evolving. What we do as a people today will be judged tomorrow by others. So culture must be free dynamic and creative. Culture at its core is about change. Culture is never limiting, it is a place where the mind grows, a place where the soul is nurtured, a place where the possibilities are limitless.

Since Belize is a multi-ethnic society, there will always be the feeling that certain cultures are better than others, but this is

a false sense of nation. Culture should go beyond race, class and religious beliefs. It should embrace the best of our human nature, the power to create and transform ourselves.

The challenge for us is to expand on our existing culture, and make it new. The best writers, painters, musicians, dancers, actors, video artists, and others must understand their culture, then transform it.

We can learn from but not surrender to the many influences we receive from the media. We must create our own culture from whatever we feel is ours since culture is the place where we free our creative forces and take control of our lives and our environment.

Chronological Table

200 - 800 A.D. -	Maya cities flourish all through Belize.
900 1000 A.D. -	Maya cultural decline in Southern and Central America
1520s -	Cortes crosses Southern Belize
1530s -	Montejo attempts to conquer Belize for Spain. Nachankan and Belize Maya defeat Spanish.
1650s -	British buccaneers begin to settle Belizean coast.
1660 -	Bartholomew Sharpe, famous British pirate, makes Belize his base and begins to harvest logwood for sale to U.K.
1670 -	Godolphin (Madrid) Treaty opening all of the Americas to British colonization.
1717 -	Spanish force from Peten drives out Baymen.
1720s -	First record of African slaves in Belize.
1754 -	Spanish drive out Baymen who return within a year.
1763 -	Treaty of Paris: Spain permitted British settlers to cut logwood; no boundaries defined.
1765 -	Admiral Burnaby codified Settlement's Regulations, known as "Burnaby's Code". Public meetings passed resolutions on boundaries of logwood works.
1765/68/73 -	Slaves revolt.
1779 -	Spanish forces capture Belize and take Baymen and slaves to Yucatan. Slaves freed after declaring loyalty to Spain. Baymen sent to Cuba.
1783 -	Treaty of Versailles: Spain recognizes British rights to cut logwood in Belize between the Hondo and Belize rivers.
1784 -	Settlers return to Belize; Despard appointed first Superintendent of the settlement.
1786 -	Convention of London expands British rights in Belize to the Sibun and permits mahogany cutting.
1787 -	British evacuate Mosquito Shore and 2,214 "Shoremen" and their slaves came to Belize. Public meeting determined qualifications for owning mahogany works.
1788 -	Maya attack mahogany works on New River.
1798 -	Battle of St. George's Caye
1802 -	150 Garifuna already settled at Stann Creek.
1807 -	Abolition of slave trade.
1817 -	Superintendent takes away power of settlers to issue lands; large body of runaway slaves reported in the interior.
1820 -	Slave revolt.
1821 -	Mexican and Central American independence.
1831 -	Act passed to give equal rights to "colored subjects" as to whites.
1832 -	Large number of Garifuna arrive in Belize (Garifuna Settlement Day).

1834/38 - Slavery abolished. Land ordered to be sold and no longer issued free.

1847 - War of the Castes in Yucatan sends thousands of refugees into Belize.

1856 - North side of Belize City destroyed by fire.

1859 - British- Guatemala Treaty over Belize. British Honduras Company (later B.E.C.) formed.

1862 - Belize becomes the Colony of "British Honduras".

1865 - Labourers brought from West Indian islands and China, especially for work on sugar estates of B.H. Co.

1866 - British troops routed by Maya in Yalbac Hills.

1867 - Reinforced British Troops destroy Maya villages and crops in Yalbac.

1871 - Belize declared Crown Colony after Assembly dissolved itself in 1870. Three of the four unofficial members in new Legislative Council represent landed interests.

1894 - Constables mutiny. Belizean workers riot for better pay.

1906 - Belize City gets electricity.

1914 - World War I - Many Belizean volunteers served.

1919 - Belizean troops riot upon return home.

1922 - Marcus Garvey visits Belize.

1929 - Great Depression begins.

1931 - Great Hurricane - over 2,000 dead.

1933 - Guatemala re-asserts claim to Belize.

1934 - Antonio Soberanis leads workers protests.

1939 - World War II.

1949 - B.H. dollar devalued.

1950 - Founding of the P.U.P.

1952 - National strike led by General Workers Union.

1954 - Vote for all adults.

1964 - Self Government.

1968 - The "Webster Proposals": Draft treaty presented by U.S.A. mediator for Anglo-Guatemalan dispute, rejected by government and people.

1970 - Belmopan becomes capital of Belize.

1970's - Internationalization of Belize's cause.

1971 - Belize Joins CARIFTA.

1973 - Country's name legally changed to "Belize". Aliens Landholding Ordinance passed.

1975 - First pro-Belize resolution passed by General Assembly of United Nations.

1976 - Belize given "special status" in Non-Aligned Movement.

1981 - Independence
Belize joins Commonwealth, United Nations and Non-Aligned Movement.

SEPTEMBER 1981
INDEPENDENCE DAY

BELIZE CENTRAL AMERICA

Words to know

Abolition - the act of ending the system of slavery.

Absentee Landlord - one who seldom visits the land he owns.

Abstain - to refrain from using one's vote.

Alliance - confederation or association of persons or states, joined for the purpose of working together.

Ancestor - forefather, ancient relation.

Apprehension - arrest, a feeling of fear about possible danger.

Archaeologist - a scientist who studies past human life through remains.

Bail - money or property pledged as security that a person accused of a crime will return, if he is released temporarily, to stand trial.

Bankrupt - a person who is unable to pay his debts in full.

Boom - floating timber barrier across water.

Boycott - the refusal to buy goods from a certain person, company or nation.

Capital - money or property that is used or invested to produce more wealth. The money with which a business etc... is started.

Capitalist - person who controls the wealth, means of production and labour in a society; the class to which such a person belongs.

Cargo - ship's freight or load.

Census - official count of the population in a given area.

Cession - ceding; transferring territory from one ruler to an other.

Civil Service - the service responsible for the public administration of the government of a country. Members of the civil service are not generally affected by the change of government.

Civil War - war between parties or inhabitants of different regions within the same nation.

Cold War - state of political hostility and military tension between two power blocs.

Colonialism - a system of external domination in which all aspects of society are controlled by another nation.

Commercial - of or for trade.

Concession(s) - something yielded or granted, given in to.

Condition(ed) - to get used to, accept, to develop a habit.

Constitution - the set of principles according to which a country is organized.

Contraband - trade in forbidden goods; smuggling.

Contract - agreement made, enforceable by law.

Co-operative(s) - joint effort of production or distribution where members share the profit.

Cultivate(d) - to prepare and use (land) for crops.

Culture(s) - the customs and civilization of a particular people or group.

Debit - charge.

Decolonization - process of no longer being a colony, becoming independent.

Deport - to remove an unwanted person from a country; to expel.

Descendant(s) - a person who comes from a certain family or people; from one generation to another.

Devaluation - reduction in the value of money.

Diplomatic - engaged in the management of international relations.

Discrimination - to make a distinction; to give unfair treatment, especially because of prejudice.

Economy - a system of using resources to produce wealth.

Elite - the privileged group of people in a society.

Emancipate(d) - free from legal, social, intellectual control; liberate from slavery.

Emigrate - go to settle in another country.

Empires - a group of countries ruled by a single supreme authority.

Entrepot trade - goods imported into a country to be exported to other countries.

Environments - surroundings, especially those affecting people's life.

Expedition(s) - journey or voyage for a definite purpose.

Exploit(ed) - to use for one's own ends; to take advantage of.

Famine - serious lack of food; starvation for a large area.

Freehold(er) - the holding of property by legal right for life.

Great Depression - the period from 1929 to 1939 of sharp decline in the production of goods and services, causing business failures, high unemployment, and poverty and a major world economic crisis.

Hemisphere - either of the half into which the Earth is divided.

Humanitarian(s) - person interested in helping people; works to better mankind.

Illiterate - not able to read and write.

Immigrant(s)- person who comes to settle in another country.

Imperial - having to do with an empire; having control over other countries, people and resources.

Incursions - a raid or brief invasion into someone else's territory.

Indentured servant(s) - person bound by contract to work for (serve) a master for a certain period of time.

Indigenous - original, first; native.

Industrial - having to do with making goods (industry); business.

Infrastructure - the installations that form the basis of an enterprise.

Inspect - to examine carefully.

Interdependent - depending on each other.

Inventory - a detailed list of goods and materials in stock.

Land tenure - the system by which land is owned or leased.

Lapse(d) - end because of disuse (not being used).

Legislative Assembly - any assembly with the powers to make laws.

Lobby - try to influence or convince a political representative or group to support your view.

Looted - goods taken by theft.

Malnutrition - not being well fed; sick from lack of proper food.

Manage - to have under effective control.

Manufacture(d) - things made; produced in large amounts for sale, using machines.

Market(s) - trade in goods; demand for goods.

Marketing - to offer for sale, to go buying food.

Maroons - escaped slaves in the West Indies who formed their own communities in the woods.

Media - newspapers, radio, television, movies - by which information is conveyed to the general public.

Mediate - to try to settle the differences between two groups.

Mesoamerica - the middle of the American continents, Central America.

Middle class - the class of society between the upper and working class, including business and professional people.

Migration - the act of moving to another area or country.

Monopolization - to take exclusive control.

Monopoly - total control over or having the sole rights to trade or provide a service.

Negotiate - to bargain or discuss; to arrange by agreement.

Neutrality - the act of not taking sides in an argument or conflict.

Open letter - a letter of comment or protest nominally addressed to a person but sent to and printed in a newspaper.

Partnership - a contract between two or more persons carrying a joint business, for profit in view, sharing losses or profits.

Perpetuity - a condition that will never end; forever.

Petition(ed) - to submit a formal application to a court of law or member of government; to make a written request or appeal.

Picket(s) - one or more workers on strike who stand outside the work place to encourage others to stop working also, as a protest.

Process(ing,ed) - a series of actions or operations used in making or manufacturing or achieving something.

Proclamation - a public statement.

Prohibition - period in U.S.A. history when alcoholic drinks were not allowed to be sold, 1920s.

Propaganda - publicity intended to spread ideas or information that will persuade or convince people.

Provisions - supplies of food.

Psychological(ly) - the way in which a person's thoughts and feelings are affected and molded by the social, economic and political systems.

Public Meeting - A body used by the British settlers for decision making during the 18th century and early 19th century.

Quota - a fixed share that must be done, contributed or received.

Raw Materials - any material or product that is processed to make another.

Re-exports - imported goods exported to another country.

Refugee(s) - person who seeks safety from danger, war; who flees to another country or area.

Regulation - a rule or restriction.

Resolution - something one intends to do.

Resources - supplies of money or raw materials; land, water minerals, or people used to produce things.

Rural - those areas of a country other that a town or city e.g. villages and farm lands or forests.

Scab - a worker who refuses to join a strike or who takes a striker's job.

Serfdom - system during the Middle Ages in Europe under which a farmer was bought and sold with the land on which he worked; he owed everything to the land owner, called the lord, who controlled the farmer's life.

Slave Labour - work done by slaves.

Sloop - a one-masted sailing ship.

Solidarity - unity in support of common interests.

Sovereignty - the supreme power of an independent state; ultimate control.

Speculated(d) - to invest money in something with the hope to earn a profit from it.

Squatter(s) - one who settles on land without legal right.

Strike - a workers' refusal to work, in protest about an imaginary or real complaint.

Subsistence farming - a type of farming in which most of the produce is consumed by the farmer and his family leaving little or nothing to be marketed.

Technologically - having to do with science for development.

Territorial integrity - total control or sovereignty of a nation over all its lands; the principle that a country should keep all its lands and not be made to give up any.

Transnational - multinational; owned and operated in or by many different countries.

Tribute - money paid by one person or nation to another regularly, in return for peace and protection.

Underdeveloped - a country not having reached its potential level in economic development.

Unemployment - situation where people are out of work; there are not enough jobs.

Universal adult suffrage - the right for all adults (over 21 or 18 depending on the law) to vote, no matter what their race, sex, religion, education or economic status.

Urban - having to do with cities and towns.

Urbanization - to change a place into a town-like area.

Working class - the class of people who are employed for wages, especially in manual or industrial work.

World War I - A war fought between nations throughout the world from 1914 to 1918, which claimed 10 million lives.

World War II - the second major war that occurred from 1939 to 1945 that claimed 50 million lives, and which ended with the surrender of Germany and the explosion of the first atomic bomb over Japan.

Index

Key

🖊 *This symbol represents an individual activity.*

🖊🖊 *This symbol represents a group activity.*